Song of Creation

Song of Creation

*An Anthology of Poems
in Praise of Animals*

Edited with an Introduction
by
Andrew Linzey and Tom Regan

Abbey
Books

Marshall Morgan and Scott
Marshall Pickering
3 Beggarwood Lane, Basingstoke, Hants RG23 7LP, UK

Copyright © 1988 A Linzey & T Regan.
First published in 1988 by Marshall Morgan and Scott
Publication Ltd
Part of the Marshall Pickering Holdings Group
A subsidiary of the Zondervan Corporation

British Library CIP Data

ISBN: 0 551 01641 8

Text Set in Baskerville by Input Typesetting Ltd,
SW19 8DR
Printed in Great Britain by
Richard Clay Ltd, Bungay, Suffolk

To

EDWARD CARPENTER

recently Dean of Westminster,
whose life-long work
for animals
has been an inspiration.

—— Contents ——

About the Editors

The Revd Dr Andrew Linzey is the foremost theologian dealing with the issue of animal rights. He has written or edited seven books specialising in Christian ethics including *Christianity and the Rights of Animals* (SPCK 1987). He is Chaplain and Director of Studies, Centre for the Study of Theology in the University of Essex and was for four years a member of the National Council of the RSPCA.

Professor Tom Regan is the intellectual leader of the animal rights movement. He is Professor of Philosophy at the North Carolina State University, President of the Culture and Animals Foundation and has written or edited eighteen books specialising in applied philosophy. He is author of *The Case for Animal Rights* (University of California Press, 1983) which is the definitive work on the subject.

Acknowledgements

Our debts are many. Our special thanks to: The Culture and Animals Foundation, USA, for an initial grant to cover some of the research costs and for their encouragement of this venture; Nicholas Garrard and Penny Fleming of Wescott House, Cambridge, for their valuable research assistance; Jon Wynne-Tyson whose own anthology, *The Extended Circle: A Dictionary of Humane Thought* (Centaur Press, 1986), is a classic in this field and who has kindly allowed us to use his extracts from John Gay, Alexander Pope, Ella Wheeler Wilcox and Oliver Goldsmith together with his own selection from the poems of Henry S Salt; Dr Peter J Wexler from the University of Essex who kindly found for us the letter from Charles Lamb to Southey; Virginia McKenna for the poem by John Galsworthy; Cindy Milburn of the RSPCA for the poem 'The Shepherd's Dog and the Wolf' by John Gay; and to the many others who made helpful suggestions.

Thanks are also due to the following for permission to quote from copyright and/or other published material: Allison & Busby/W H Allen Publishers for Adrian Mitchell's 'Back in the Playground Blues' and 'What Became of Them?' from the *Kingfisher Book of Children's Poetry*; Laurence Pollinger Ltd and the Estate of Mrs Frieda Lawrence Ravagli for 'Snake', 'Mountain Lion' and 'Lizard' by D H Lawrence; Virginia McKenna for her poem 'Solitude'; *The Radio Times* and Roger Woddis for his poem 'The Smell of Money'; Jon Wynne-Tyson, literary executor, for his selection from H S Salt's poetry originally published in CVM GRANO, Oriole Press, 1931, and for his own copyright poems 'The Shooting Party', 'Down the Road Two Humans have been Murdered' and 'Dog'; Myfanwy Thomas for her father, Edward Thomas's poem 'The Gallows'; Armorel Kay Walling for her poems 'Go Tell All Creatures in the World', 'Easter' and 'Vesper'; J M Dent & Sons Ltd Publishers for 'The Praise of Created Things' by St Francis of Assisi and 'The Donkey' by G K Chesterton; Chatto & Windus and the Hogarth Press for the extract from 'Isabella' by John Keats; the Division of Christian Education of the National Council of the Churches of Christ in the USA for quotations from the Revised Standard Version of the Bible, copyrighted 1952 and 1971; Marshall Pickering for 'Lamb on the Anelog Mountain' and 'Cosmic Prayer (i) and (ii)' by Brother Ramon, SSF, from *A Hidden Fire*; Routledge and Kegan Paul Publishers (Associated Book Publishers, UK, Ltd) for 'The Birds' and extracts from 'Woodnotes' from *Poems* by R W Emerson; also 'The Nightingale and the Glow-worm', 'On A Goldfinch Starved to Death in a Cage', 'The Cockfighter's Garland', 'Epigram', 'Epitaph on Flop', extracts from 'The Garden' and 'The Winter Walk at Noon' from William Cowper's *Works*; Macmillan and Company Ltd for 'A Butcher' and 'On Richard Martin' by Thomas Hood — the latter in *Valiant Crusade* by A W Moss; also to Macmillan for extract from 'In Memoriam' by Alfred, Lord Tennyson, 'On the Death of a Favourite Canary' by Matthew Arnold from F T Palgrave (ed.), *The Golden Treasury*, and 'Last Words to a Dumb Friend', 'The Puzzled Game-Birds', 'A Sheep Fair', 'Bags of Meat', 'The Blinded Bird', 'Compassion', 'The Lady in Furs' and 'The Mongrel' all in Thomas Hardy, *The Complete Poems*, also to Macmillan for 'The White Tiger' by R S Thomas from *Frequencies*; Grafton Books, a division of Collins Publishing Group, for 'To a Starved Hare', 'On Shooting a Swallow', 'The Cattle Train', 'Cynotaphium' and 'Silent Praise' from *A Hundred Sonnets* by Charles Tennyson Turner; Gibbings and Company for extracts from 'Jocelyn's Episode' by A de Lamartine and 'On the Death of a Favourite Spaniel' by Robert Southey both from J G Wood, *Man and Beast: Here and Hereafter*; Penguin Books for 'The Dead Sparrow' by William Cartwright, 'The Marvellous Bear Shepherd,' 'The Lamb' and 'The Tiger' by William Blake and 'Canticle to the Waterbirds' by Brother Antoninus from *The Penguin Book of Animal Verse*; also for 'Auguries of Innocence' by William Blake, extract from 'The Rime of the Ancient Mariner' by S T Coleridge, and extracts from 'Lines' and 'Lines written in Early Spring' by William Wordsworth from *The Penguin Book of English Romantic Verse*; also for extract from 'Windsor Forest' by Alexander Pope and extract from 'Winter' by Robert Bloomfield from *The Penguin Book of Eighteenth Century English*

Verse; also for extract from 'Song of Myself' by Walt Whitman in *The Penguin Whitman*; for 'On the Death of a Monkey' by Thomas Heyrick from *The Metaphysical Poets*, and for 'To the Humble-Bee' by R W Emerson from *The Centuries' Poetry*; Oxford University Press for poetry from Byron, Donne, Hopkins, Longfellow, Shelley, Vaughan, Whittier and Wordsworth which appear in their collected editions; Victor Gollancz Ltd for 'Miracles' by Walt Whitman from *A Year of Grace* compiled by Victor Gollancz; Alan Brownjohn for his poem 'We are Going to See the Rabbit'; David Higham Associates Ltd for 'Still Falls the Rain' by Edith Sitwell from *Collected Poems* published by Macmillan; J M Dent & Sons Ltd for 'The Robin', 'To the Snipe', extract from 'The Parish: A Satire', 'Nature's Hymn to Deity', 'The Badger' and 'The Mole-Catcher' by John Clare from *Selected Poems* edited by J & A Tibble; Darton, Longman and Todd for 'A Hymn to God the Creator' extract from *Love's Endeavour, Love's Expense* by W H Vanstone; Lion Publishing for 'Christ's Bounties' by Tadhg, translated by K H Jackson in *A Celtic Miscellany* and reprinted by permission of Routledge and Kegan Paul; Og O Huiginn from *The Lion Book of Famous Prayers*; Saiom Bertsch for her poems 'Christian Cockroaches' and 'Number Forty One', Patrick Huddie for his 'Haydn's Creation' and 'Traveller,' and Martin Secker for Joseph Plunkett's 'I See His Blood upon the Rose' from *Selections from Modern Poets*, edited by J C Squire.

Every possible effort has been made to establish and locate copyright holders. For any omissions we apologise. We shall be glad to be notified of any oversight on our part so that errors can be rectified in any future editions of the book.

A L and T R

I love these sort of poems, that open a new intercourse with the most despised of the animal and insect race. I think this vein may be further opened; Peter Pindar hath very prettily apostrophised a fly; Burns hath his mouse and his louse; Coleridge, less successfully, hath made overtures of intimacy to a jackass, therein only following at unresembling distance Sterne and greater Cervantes. Besides these, I know of no other examples of breaking down the partition between us and our 'poor earth-bound companions.' It is sometimes revolting to be put in a track of feeling by other people, not one's own immediate thoughts, else I would persuade you, if I could (I am in earnest), to commence a series of these animal poems, which might have a tendency to rescue some poor creatures from the antipathy of mankind.

Letter of Charles Lamb to Southey, March 20, 1799, in *The Letters of Charles and Mary Anne Lamb*, Cornell University Press, 1975, p. 165.

Introduction

Those of us who care about animals are often accused of being 'emotional.' Imagine that: our being 'emotional' is an *accusation*! This tells us more about our accusers than it does about us. And what it tells us about them is that they have lost, or are desperate to repress, something that is as essential to human life as breathing itself.

For we humans are beings who feel, no less than ones who think. Our ways of relating to and comprehending the world are as much a matter of our emotional responses to it as they are cognitions of it. In the jargon of the day, we have a right-brain, not just a left-brain. It is true that we can theorise about the universe and analyse its parts. Pure reason has its place. But it is equally true that we can feel ourself-in-relation-to the world and its inhabitants, in either positive or negative ways. Empathy or estrangement, at-one-ness or alienation, joy or fear, wonder or disgust — all these and more are ways in which people can and do relate emotionally to the earth and its communities of life. Those who 'accuse' others of 'being emotional' may be like colour blind people who criticise others because they marvel at shades of purple and burnt orange. Our lives are the richer, and the better (in most cases at least), for having feelings in them — and for having them expressed. Of course it is necessary to distinguish between 'higher' and 'lower' feelings or between emotions of hatred and love. Not all feelings are essentially positive.

Poetry, however, is the language of our highest feeling. It is the vehicle of common speech raised and refined to express the deepest human sentiments that might otherwise elude us. It was the English poet, William Wordsworth, who defined poetry as 'the spontaneous overflow of powerful emotion recollected in tranquillity.' Like all definitions of the complex, Wordsworth's no doubt fails to capture everything that is true of poetry. But it does get at the essence of what is best. The expression of feeling is central ('powerful emotion'). But it is feeling felt in conditions that are themselves emotionless (feelings 'recollected in tranquillity'). Which is why those emotions that *are* felt, are so compelling: they simply cannot be denied (they are 'spontaneous,' they 'overflow'). Poetry, one might say, is the language a whole human being cannot help but speak, and the emotions expressed are those a whole human being cannot help but feel.

Again, this is not to suppose that all emotions are good or by themselves sufficient for moral discourse. The very need for rational reflection is built into the art of poetry in the way 'powerful emotion' is 'recollected', that is, assessed, analysed, and refined. But notwithstanding the vital place of rational thought in moral evaluations, Christians in particular should be the first to champion the gift — for it is nothing less — of feeling. It is God who has created us feeling beings, no less than rational ones. That we can feel at all, especially that we can feel passionately and compassionately about the world is a remarkable tribute to a God who is himself the fountainhead of all love and compassion. He allows us, in other words, to feel with him, the pain and suffering of the creation he has made.

Especially in the world in which most of us live today — crowded, urban, the wildlife all but gone, city parks the last gesture to our roots in nature — especially in this world it is difficult to experience the ties that bind us to our next of kin: the animals. While we work to save the whales and protect the California condor, we fail to see that it is us, we humans, who are *the* most endangered species. Having lost the daily opportunities to interact with animals and nature generally, we are in danger of surviving only as half of what we can be: a species whose members think but do not feel. *Star Trek*'s Mr Spock may yet emerge as our species' prototype.

If there is a way to save us from ourselves, to help us reclaim our wholeness, it must include our rediscovery of our poetic heritage. For much of this poetry is about animals. And this simple fact tells us a great deal about what a whole human being is.

What it tells us is that a whole human being is incapable of denying a whole range of positive feelings about animals. These feelings include sympathy, tenderness, compassion, mercy, kindness, admiration, respect, wonder, awe, and love. Those who attain the wholeness of being human realise the

2

larger wholeness of all creatures, which is why those feelings others limit to humans only (love, mercy, and compassion, for example) are extended beyond what are often the arbitrary constraints of species' membership. And cannot help but be extended.

Henry Wadsworth Longfellow realised this. In his poem *The Birds of Killingworth* we read the following lines, spoken on behalf of saving birds from torment and death:

'How can I teach your children gentleness,
And mercy to the weak, and reverence,
For Life, which, in its weakness or excess,
Is still a gleam of God's omnipotence,
Or Death, which seeming darkness, is no less
The self-same light, although averted hence,
When by your laws, your actions, and your speech,
You contradict the very things I teach?'

Our practices as adults (our 'laws . . . actions . . . and speech') stand in the way of instructing our children in the ways of a whole human being. To teach 'gentleness' and 'mercy' is impossible so long as we do not honour these virtues in our own life. In 'weakness or excess' we do well to remember that all life still gleams with 'God's omnipotence.'

Of course, it is not only animals who are 'weak' and there-fore subject to the greatest abuse. We all recall how brutal the playground could be, and how those least able to defend themselves were most likely to be abused. Adrian Mitchell recreates the scene in these words from his poem, *Back in the Playground Blues*:

You get it for being Jewish
Get it for being black
Get it for being chicken
Get it for fighting back
You get it for being big and fat
Get it for being small
O those who get it get it and get it
for any damn thing at all

And as for the animals:

3

Sometimes they take a beetle, tear off its six legs one by
one
Beetle on its black back rocking in the lunchtime sun
But a beetle can't beg for mercy a beetle's not half the fun

'A beetle can't beg for mercy': that very incapacity to plead
for consideration is what sometimes moves us most, when
faced with animal suffering. It is what Ella Wheeler Wilcox
calls 'The sorrow that has no speech' (*Kinship*). This is the
poem that begins with these memorable lines:

I am the voice of the voiceless;
Through me the dumb shall speak,
Till the deaf world's ears be made to hear
The wrongs of the wordless weak.

Many have spoken on behalf of the 'wordless weak.' When
we read some of what has been said, we can take some comfort
in the knowledge that 'the wrongs' depicted no longer are
part of our daily life. When Robert Bloomfield writes of the
ploughman's horse that

. . . hears the whip; the chaise is at the door: . . .
The collar tightens, and again he feels
His half-healed wounds inflamed; again the wheels
With tiresome sameness in his ears resound,
O'er blinding dust, or miles of flinty ground
Thus nightly robbed, and injured day by day,
His piece-meal murderers wear his life away.
(From *Winter*)

——when we read these moving lines we may allow ourselves
the pleasure that comes from knowing that this use of animals,
as beasts of burden, is not one of those 'actions' we today
customarily visit upon the weak.

Not so in the case of other terminal interactions humans
have with animals. Hunting and other blood sports, for
example. Here both our 'laws' and 'actions' are in conflict
with the voices of our poets. William Cowper, for example,
writes:

4

                    Detested sport,
That owes its pleasures to another's pain,
That feeds upon the sobs and dying shrieks
Of harmless nature, dumb, but yet endured
With eloquence, that agonies inspire,
Of silent tears and heart distending sighs!
                    (From *The Garden*)

And Thomas Hardy, one of the greatest writers in the English language, describes the predicament of birds bred only for summary destruction:

> They are not those who used to feed us
> When we were young – they cannot be –
> These shapes that now bereave and bleed us?
> They are not those who used to feed us,
> For did we then cry, they would heed us.
> – If hearts can house such treachery
> They are not those who used to feed us
> When we were young – they cannot be!
>   (*The Puzzled Game-Birds*)

Perhaps Hardy was right in another sense too. It may be that humans can only be described as 'shapes' (that 'bereave and bleed' the animal creation) if we have not enough humanity within us to desist from wanton destruction. But it is not only on the hunting field that we can discover only 'shapes' of humanity. It is difficult to see how there can be any poetry that celebrates what we have grown accustomed to: the zoo, the laboratory, the horrors of the slaughterhouse. R. S. Thomas, in his poem *The White Tiger*, depicts the slow death of a once noble animal imprisoned in captivity:

> . . . a body too huge
> and majestic for the cage in which
> it had been put; up
> and down in the shadow
>
> of its own bulk it went,
> lifting, as it turned,
> the crumpled flower of its face.

This theme is even more sharply developed by John Galsworthy who describes a similar imprisonment:

I knew a little Serval cat –
   Never get out!
Would pad all day from this to that –
   Never get out!
From bar to bar she'd turn and turn,
   And in her eyes a fire would burn –
   (From her, Zoology we learn!)
   Never get out!
     (From *A Little Serval Cat*)

Many people take their children to see such animals. And what do they learn? Less about what a real tiger or other wild animal is like, and more about how parents 'contradict the very things' their children should be learning.

As for our use of animals in science, who can be pleased to learn that one's own friend, one's cat or dog, might die in agony at the hands of the experimenter — a practice still legally permitted in more than three-fourths of the states in the United States. Where is the love and compassion, that loyalty and pity when, with the narrator in Robert Browning's poem *Tray*, a human voice declares:

'John, go and catch — or, if needs be,
Purchase that animal for me!
By vivisection, at expense
Of half-an-hour and eighteenpence,
How brain secretes dog's soul, we'll see!'

And lest we think that Browning's imagination is over-active on the matter of how animals are used in science, it is important to recall a description of actual practice from an earlier time and place. The Cartesian scientists of Port Royal, it is said by a contemporary of theirs:

administered beatings to dogs with perfect indifference and made fun of those who pitied the creatures as if they felt pain. They said that animals were clocks; that the cries they emitted when struck were only the noise of a little spring that had been touched, and that the whole body was without feeling. They nailed the poor animals up on boards by their four paws to vivisect them to see the circulation of the blood which was a great subject of controversy.

If today we reject the Cartesian teaching that 'the whole body (of an animal) is without feeling,' our guilt is compounded, not reduced. For the sake of the adornment of *our* human bodies the bodies of animals are mutilated. Saiom Bertsch in her poem *Number Forty One* describes the torment that animals must suffer for the sake of procuring a small amount of musk:

was it misnumbered?
this perfume numbered five?
take 1 part of ambergris
from a sperm whale
add some drops of castor
ripped from a Canadian beaver
and 1 civet cat rotated
in a drum to frighten it
into secreting hormones
and 38 musk oxen castrated
for 1 ounce of musk
. . . should this perfume
be called Perfume No. 41?

And we must not stop here. Christian compassion must also extend to those animals bred, reared (more often than not in cruel intensive conditions) and transported in order to satisfy our demand for cheap meat. Charles Tennyson Turner describes how the beauty of a summer's day was disturbed:

When, suddenly, a cattle-train went by,
Rapt, in a moment, from, my pitying eye,
As from their loving mates in Irish vales;
Close-pack'd and mute they stood, as close as bees,
Bewilder'd with their fright and narrow room;
'Twas sad to see the meek-eyed hecatomb,
So fiercely hurried past our summer seas,
Our happy bathers, and our fresh sea-breeze,
And hills of blooming heather, to their doom.
(From *The Cattle Train*)

Any view of animals that sees them just as means to our ends, as simply resources to utilise or indeed as just 'bags of meat' – as Thomas Hardy describes it — represents a deeply impoverished view of creation. The greed of humankind is nowhere better characterised than in Hardy's poem describing a cattle auction:

> Each beast, when driven in,
> Looks round at the ring of bidders there
> With a much-amazed reproachful stare,
> As at unnatural kin,
> For bringing him to a sinister scene
> So strange, unhomelike, hungry, mean;
> His fate the while suspended between
> A butcher, to kill out of hand,
> And a farmer, to keep on the land;
> One can fancy a tear runs down his face
> When the butcher wins, and he's driven from the place.
>
> (From *Bags of Meat*)

With such a dismal record of respect and love, with so little to be said for human compassion and pity, it is small wonder that some people are sorely tempted to raise the rest of the animal creation above, not demand that it be placed below, the position we humans occupy in the great chain of being. Mark Twain was so inclined. Recall his observation that 'in studying the traits and dispositions of the so-called lower animals, and contrasting them with man's, I find the result humiliating to me . . . Of all the creatures ever made he [man] is the most detestable.' John Gay would agree. In his moving poem, *An Elegy on a Lap Dog*, about a dog named Shock, Gay concludes with this memorable couplet:

> *Here* Shock, *the pride of all his kind, is laid;*
> *Who fawn'd like man, but ne'er like man betrayed.*

This theme, of the ingratitude and disloyalty of humans, and the superior moral qualities of other animals, is one that is played out again and again in poetry, but perhaps nowhere with greater power than in these lines from Byron's *Inscription on the Monument of a Newfoundland Dog*:

8

When some proud son of man returns to earth,
Unknown to glory, but upheld by birth,
The sculptor's art exhausts the pomp of woe,
And storied urns record who rest below:
When all is done, upon the tomb is seen,
Not what he was, but what he should have been:
But the poor dog, in life the firmest friend,
The first to welcome, foremost to defend,
Whose honest heart is still his master's own,
Who labours, fights, lives, breathes for him alone,
Unhonour'd falls, unnoticed all his worth,
Denied in heaven the soul he held on earth:
While man, vain insect! hopes to be forgiven,
And claims himself a sole exclusive heaven.

Is there no middle way, then, between the vision of humans-as-superior and humans-as-inferior? Must one species always come first? The rest, last?

Perhaps there is a middle way, one in which the beauty and dignity of all God's creatures, humans and animals, can be recognised and respected. This is the way envisioned in religious images by Brother Antoninus in his long poem, *A Canticle for the Waterbirds: Written for the Feast of St Francis of Assisi, 1950*, one part of which reads as follows:

You leave a silence. And this for you suffices, who are not of the ceremonials of man,
And hence are not made sad to now forgo them.
Yours is of another order of being, and wholly it compels.
But you may, birds, utterly seized in God's supremacy,
Austerely living under His austere eye –
Yet may you teach a man a necessary thing to know,
Which has to do if the strict conformity that creaturehood entails,
And constitutes the prime commitment all things share.
For God has given you the imponderable grace to *be* His verification,
Outside the mulled incertitude of our forensic choices;
That you, our lessers in the rich hegemony of Being,
May serve as testament to what a creature is,
And what creation owes.

An even stronger vision of fraternity and mutuality between creatures is expressed by the great Scottish poet, Robert Burns. In a number of poems, he first regrets the severed ties of trust between humans and animals, and then affirms his hope of future harmony or restoration. Here are two examples:

Why, ye tenants of the lake,
For me your watery haunt forsake?
Tell me, fellow-creatures, why
At my presence thus you fly?
Why disturb your social joys,
Parent, filial, kindred ties?
Common friend to you and me,
Nature's gifts to all are free:
Peaceful keep your dimpling wave,
Busy feed, or wanton lave;
Or, beneath thy sheltering rock,
Bide the surging billow's shock.
                    (From *On Scaring some Waterfowl in Loch-Truit*)

And, the second example, this one from his famous poem, *To A Mouse*:

Wee, sleekit, cowrin', tim'rous beastie,
Oh, what a panic's in thy breastie!
Thou needna start awa'sae hasty,
     Wi' bickring brattle!
I wad laith to rin and chase thee,
     Wi' mud'ring pattle!
I'm truly sorry man's dominion
Has broken nature's social union,
And justifies that ill opinion
     Which mak's thee startle
At me, thy poor earth-born companion,
     And fellow-mortal!

This hope for a time when humans and animals will live in peace without violence has deep roots within the Judeo-Christian tradition. For this reason alone we have found it essential to include some of the earliest poetry found in the Old Testament notably in the psalms and also in the prophetic books such as Isaiah. For here especially we find a vision of perfect harmony and coexistence when all things shall be redeemed:

> The wolf shall dwell with the lamb,
> and the leopard shall lie down with the kid,
> and the calf and the fatling together,
> and a little child shall lead them . . .
>
> They shall not hurt or destroy
> in all my holy mountain:
> for the earth shall be full of the knowledge
> of the Lord
> as the waters cover the sea.
> (*Isaiah 11: 1–9*)

The New Testament too does not abandon this hope. In St Paul's letter to the Church in Rome, he makes it clear that while the whole creation suffers now, like a woman in labour, these pains are a precursor to a new birth which will involve the whole creation in a new freedom. 'For the creation waits with eager longing,' writes St Paul, 'for the revealing of the sons of God.' These people, who are nothing less than inspired human beings who have themselves been redeemed, are to help creation to become free. '(B)ecause the creation itself will be set free from its bondage to decay and obtain the glorious liberty of the children of God.' (*Romans 8: 18–23*). Perhaps no poet has ever described the task before us more vividly than St Paul in these words.

Thus does the language of poetry speak — always and everywhere in the language of love and compassion, of a sense of loss and the longing for restoration. Like it or not, we have failed in our great challenge to be compassionate of all and, in so doing, to find the way to the fullness that is our God-given nature. These are the themes which 'powerful emotion' poetry about animals embodies and in which we find the promise of enrichment. For it is not only the animals, or nature alone, that is impoverished and abused by our species' thirst for supremacy and domination. In this case the 'conquerors' are among the real victims. *We* are the less for having treated, and for continuing to treat, our fellow animals as less. As Abraham Lincoln saw, to be 'in favour of animal rights as well as human rights . . . is the way of a whole human

11

being.' And that is the way of the earth's renewal, too, as Brother Ramon, SSF, states in the final lines of this anthology:

> So men of God are drawn to prayer
> By the indwelling Spirit's call,
> And men of faith and love arise
> Reversing thus the cosmic fall;
> Redeeming man's aridity,
> Renewing earth's fertility.
> (From *The Bondage of Creation*)

These, then, are some of the themes, and a few of the actual poems, that lie ahead. They make for more than good reading. They offer edification and inspiration, vision and — not the least of all virtues, hope. That hope is simple. We *can* do better. And we *will*. Nothing less than a whole human life, and the wholeness of the lives of our fellow creatures, hangs in the balance. Only then perhaps shall we be able to sing the song of creation.

Psalm

[104: 5–30]

Thou Didst set the Earth on its Foundations

Thou didst set the earth on its foundations,
   so that it should never be shaken.
Thou didst cover it with the deep as with a garment;
   the waters stood above the mountains.
At thy rebuke they fled;
   at the sound of thy thunder they took to flight.
The mountains rose, the valleys sank down
   to the place which thou didst appoint for them.
Thou didst set a bound which they should not pass,
   so that they might not again cover the earth.

Thou makest springs gush forth in the valleys;
   they flow between the hills,
   they give drink to every beast of the field;
   the wild asses quench their thirst.
By them the birds of the air have their habitation;
   they sing among the branches.
From thy lofty above thou waterest the mountains;
   the earth is satisfied with the fruit of thy work.

Thou dost cause the grass to grow for the cattle,
   and plants for man to cultivate,
that he may bring forth food from the earth,
   and wine to gladden the heart of man,
oil to make his face shine,
   and bread to strengthen man's heart.
The trees of the LORD are watered abundantly,
   the cedars of Lebanon which he planted.
In them the birds build their nests;

the stork has her home in the fir trees.
The high mountains are for the wild goats;
   the rocks are a refuge for the badgers.
Thou hast made the moon to mark the seasons;
   the sun knows its time for setting.
Thou makest darkness, and it is night,
   when all the beasts of the forest creep forth.
The young lions roar for their prey,
   seeking their food from God.
When the sun rises, they get them away
   and lie down in their dens.
Man goes forth to his work
   and to his labour until the evening.
O LORD, how manifold are thy works!
   In wisdom hast thou made them all;
   the earth is full of thy creatures.
Yonder is the sea, great and wide,
   which teems with things innumerable,
   living things both small and great.
There go the ships, and Levi'athan
   which thou didst form to sport in it.

These all look to thee,
   to give them their food in due season.
When thou givest to them, they gather it up;
   when thou openest thy hand,
   they are filled with good things.
When thou hidest thy face, they are dismayed;
   when thou takest away their breath, they die
   and return to their dust.
When thou sendest forth thy Spirit, they are created;
   and thou renewest the face of the ground.

Psalm

[148: 3–13]

Praise Him Sun and Moon

Praise him, sun and moon,
 praise him, all you shining stars!
Praise him, you highest heavens,
 and you waters above the heavens!

Let them praise the name of the Lord!
 For he commanded and they were created.
And he established them for ever and ever;
 he fixed their bounds which cannot be passed.

Praise the Lord from the earth,
 you sea monsters and all deeps,
fire and hail, snow and frost,
 stormy wind fulfilling his command!

Mountains and all hills,
 fruit trees and all cedars!
Beasts and all cattle,
 creeping things and flying birds!

Kings of the earth and all peoples,
 princes and all rulers of the earth!
Young men and maidens together,
 old men and children!

Let them praise the name of the Lord,
for his name alone is exalted;
his glory is above earth and heaven.

15

—— JOB ——

[40: 6–42]

Then the Lord answered Job

Then the Lord answered Job out of the whirlwind:
    'Gird up your loins like a man;
  I will question you, and you declare to me.
Will you even put me in the wrong?
    Will you condemn me that you may be justified?
  Have you an arm like God,
    and can you thunder with a voice like his?

Deck yourself with majesty and dignity;
  clothe yourself with glory and splendour.
Pour forth the overflowings of your anger,
  and look on every one that is proud, and abase him.
Look on every one that is proud, and bring him low;
  and tread down the wicked where they stand.
Hide them all in the dust together;
  bind their faces in the world below.
Then will I also acknowledge to you,
  that your own right hand can give you victory.
Behold, Be'hemoth,
  which I made as I made you; he eats grass like an ox.
Behold, his strength in his loins,
  and his power in the muscles of his belly.
He makes his tail stiff like a cedar;
  the sinews of his thighs are knit together.
His bones are tubes of bronze,
  his limbs like bars of iron.

He is the first of the works of God;
  let him who made him bring near his sword!

For the mountains yield food for him
  where all the wild beasts play.
Under the lotus plants he lies,
  in the covert of the reeds and in the marsh.
For his shade the lotus trees cover him;
  the willows of the brook surround him.
Behold, if the river is turbulent he is not frightened;
  he is confident though Jordan rushes against his mouth.
Can one take him with hooks, or pierce his nose with a snare?

Can you draw out Levi'athan with a fishook,
  or press down his tongue with a cord?
Can you put a rope in his nose,
  or pierce his jaw with a hook?
Will he make many supplications to you?
Will he speak to you soft words?
Will he make a covenant with you to take him for your
    servant for ever?
Will you play with him as with a bird,
  or will you put him on leash for your maidens?
Will traders bargain over him?
  Will they divide him up among the merchants?
Can you fill his skin with harpoons,
  or his head with fishing spears?
Lay hands on him;
  think of the battle; you will not do it again!
Behold, the hope of a man is disappointed;
  he is laid low even at the sight of him.
No one is so fierce that he dares to stir him up.
  Who then is he that can stand before me?
Who has given to me, that I should repay him?
  Whatever is under the whole heaven is mine.

I will not keep silence concerning his limbs,
  or his mighty strength, or his goodly frame.
Who can strip off his outer garment?
  Who can penetrate his double coat of mail?
Who can open the doors of his face?
  Round about his teeth is terror.
His back is made of rows of shields,
  shut up closely as with a seal.

One is so near to another
    that no air can come between them.
They are joined one to another;
    they clasp each other and cannot be separated.
His sneezings flash forth light,
    and his eyes are like the eyelids of the dawn.
Out of his mouth go flaming torches;
    sparks of fire leap forth.
Out of his nostrils comes forth smoke,
    as from a boiling pot and burning rushes.
His breath kindles coals,
    and a flame comes forth from his mouth.
In his neck abides strength,
    and terror dances before him.
The folds of his flesh cleave together,
    firmly cast upon him and immovable.
His heart is hard as a stone,
    hard as the nether millstone.
When he raises himself up the mighty are afraid;
    at the crashing they are beside themselves.
Though the sword reaches him,
    it does not avail
    nor the spear, the dart, or the javelin.
He counts iron as straw,
    and bronze as rotten wood.
The arrow cannot make him flee;
    for him slingstones are turned to stubble.
Clubs are counted as stubble;
    he laughs at the rattle of javelins.
His underparts are like sharp potsherds;
    he spreads himself like a threshing sledge on the mire.
He makes the deep boil like a pot;
    he makes the sea like a pot of ointment.
Behind him he leaves a shining wake;
    one would think the deep to be hoary.
Upon earth there is not his like,
    a creature without fear.
He beholds everything that is high;
    he is king over all the sons of pride.'

Isaiah

[11: 1–9]

There shall come forth a shoot

There shall come forth a shoot from the stump of Jesse,
    and a branch shall grow out of his roots.
And the Spirit of the Lord shall rest upon him,
    the spirit of wisdom and understanding,
    the spirit of counsel and might,
    the spirit of knowledge and the fear of the Lord.
And his delight shall be in the fear of the Lord.

He shall not judge by what his eyes see,
    or decide by what his ears hear;
but with righteousness he shall judge the poor,
    and decide with equity for the meek of the earth;
and he shall smite the earth with the rod of his mouth,
    and with the breath of his lips he shall slay the wicked.
Righteousness shall be the girdle of his waist,
    and faithfulness the girdle of his loins.
The wolf shall dwell with the lamb,
    and the leopard shall lie down with the kid,
and the calf and the lion and the fatling together,
    and a little child shall lead them.
The cow and the bear shall feed;
    their young shall lie down together;
    and the lion shall eat straw like the ox.
The sucking child shall play over the hole of the asp,
    and the weaned child shall put his hand on the adder's den.
They shall not hurt or destroy
    in all my holy mountain:
for the earth shall be full of the knowledge of the Lord
    as the waters cover the sea.

Wisdom of Solomon

[11:24–12:1]

For Thou lovest all things that exist

For thou lovest all things that exist,
and hast loathing for none of the things
which thou hast made,
for thou wouldst not have made anything
if thou hadst hated it.
How could anything endure if thou didst not will it?
Or how could anything not called by thee be preserved?
Thou sparest all things, for they are thine,
O Lord who lovest the living,
and thy immortal spirit is in all things.

St Paul

Romans 8: 18–23

I consider that the sufferings of the present time
are not worth comparing with the glory
that is to be revealed to us.
For the creation waits with eager longing
for the revealing of the sons of God;
for the creation was subject to futility,
not of its own will

20

but by the will of him
who subjected it in hope;
because the creation itself will be set free
from its bondage to decay
and obtain the glorious liberty
of the children of God.
We know that the whole creation
has been groaning in travail
together until now.

—— St Francis of Assisi ——

[c. 1181–1226]

The Praise of Created Things

Most High, Omnipotent, Good Lord.
Thine be the praise, the glory, the honour, and all
benediction.
To Thee alone, Most High, they are due,
and no man is worthy to mention Thee.

Be Thou praised, my Lord, with all Thy creatures,
above all Brother Sun,
who gives the day and lightens us therewith.

And he is beautiful and radiant with great splendour,
of Thee, Most High, he bears similitude.

Be Thou praised, my Lord, of Sister Moon and the stars,
in the heaven hast Thou formed them, clear and precious
and comely.

Be Thou praised, my Lord, of Brother Wind,
and of the air, and the cloud, and of fair and of all weather,
by the which Thou givest to Thy creatures sustenance.

Be Thou praised, my Lord, of Sister Water,
    which is much useful and humble and precious and pure.

Be Thou praised, my Lord, of Brother Fire,
    by which Thou has lightened the night,
    and he is beautiful and joyful and robust and strong.

Be Thou praised, my Lord, of our Sister Mother Earth,
    which sustains and hath us in rule,
    and produces divers fruits with coloured flowers and herbs.

Be Thou praised, my Lord, of those who pardon for Thy
    love
    and endure sickness and tribulations.

Blessed are they who will endure it in peace,
    for by Thee, Most High, they shall be crowned.

Be Thou praised, my Lord, of our Sister Bodily Death,
    from whom no man living may escape.
    woe to those who die in mortal sin:

Blessed are they who are found in Thy most holy will,
    for the second death shall not work them ill.

Praise ye and bless my Lord, and give Him thanks,
    and serve Him with great humility.

—— Tadhg Og O Huiginn ——

[?–1448]

Christ's Bounties

O Son of God, do a miracle for me, and change my
heart; thy having taken flesh to redeem me was more
difficult than to transform my wickedness.

It is thou, who to help me, didst go to be scourged . . .
thou, dear child of Mary, art the refined molten metal
   of our forge.
It is thou who makest the sun bright, together with the ice;
it is thou who createdst the rivers, and the salmon all
   along the river.
That the nut-tree should be flowering, O Christ, it is
   a rare craft; through thy skill too comes the kernel,
   thou fair ear of our wheat.
Though the children of Eve ill deserve the bird-flocks and
   salmon, it was the Immortal One on the cross who
   made both salmon and birds.
It is he who makes the flower of the sloes grow through
   the surface of the blackthorn, and the nut-flower on
   other trees; beside this, what miracle is greater?

—— **Anon (Mediaeval)** ——

The Marvellous Bear Shepherd

There were two men of holy will
  who lived together without an ill,
All lonely in a hermitage,
As meek as birdes in a cage.
The one was called Eutucylus
The other hight Florentius.
Eutucylus he was the clerke
He taught the people Goddes werk.
Florens he had much less of lore,
But in prayer wrought ever more.
Beside the house an abbey lie
Whereat in time the abbot die.

*Eutucylus
and
Florentius*

23

Then alle the monks took them to rede
To choose who should reign in his stede,
And chose for them Eutucylus
To be the abbot of their house.
Upon all hands fell the lot
So Eutucylus was made abbot.
When he was gone Florens gan dwell

Florens is
left alone

Lonely and wistful in his cell;
Withouten brother he made moan
For that he should dwell alone,
And had great sorrow and was dreary
As be they who lose good company.
And prayed he God, that he would have
Some good comforts of His love.
Thus prayed Florens by his bede

He prays God
to send him
fellowship

That Gode should send hym felauhede.
Thus prayed Florens by his bede
He prayed dere Gode of Hymn take hede
And rising up and looking out
He saw a bere, wild and stout.
This bere he came unto the gate
He came to where Florens he sate,

A bear comes
and greets him

And when the bere he comes him mere
The bere him louted and made fair cheer;
Such fair cheer as a bere might make
And asked meek he would him take.
At this Florens him bethought
That God had heard what he besought
And thanked him of his sweet grace
That he had sent him such solace,
For a miracle he must understand
That a wild bere came so tame to hand.
Now Florens he had six sheep
But no herdsmen them to keep,

And is set
to keep the
sheep

So bade the bere that he should go
And drive his sheepe to and fro.
'And kepe them well that none them tear
And thou shalt be my goode bere.'
The bere him louted with semblence glad
For to do what Florens bade,
So to the bere he gave advice;
'Every day when I eat twice

24

Come thou home at high undurne
And no longer in the field sojourne!
And every day when I fast
At the nones come home at last.'
So did the bere every day,
Nere one hour past he away,
But came he home unto the cell
Always at both times he knew well.
Then Florens had comfort and gain
Of his bere that was so tame,
And loved him much withouten fail
For the miracle and the mervaile;
    And, sooth to say, to him appeared
The bere was a most marvellous herd.
A bere through kinde should ete sheep
Yet here as herd he did them keep,
And the miracle might not be hid
The whole country knew it was did
That Florens had a tame bere
That of his sheep the herdsmen were.
The Abbot that was Eutucylus
Had four disciples envious
That all day of this bere they spake,
With keep intent evil to make,
And said all four of them between
That it was great evil scorne and mean;
'More mervail did Florentius
Than doth our abbot Eutucylus,'
They said 'that it shall not go so,'
And made forward that bere to slo.
As they said, so evil wrought,
And the dere bere to death they brought.

At evening time the bere came not.
Florens had thereof much thought
He rose and sped him to the field
And after his bere faste behelde,
And at last his bere he found,
Beside his sheep, slain, on the ground.

Then had Florens wroth and wo,
To know of evil that was so,

the first
prayer
time (for
early days)
the last
prayer
time (for
late days)

The
envious
disciples

make ready to
slay the bear

Florens looks
for his
bear

And plained him sore for his own dere
That they had slain his goode bere.
Hopeless he plained him wondrous sore,
That his solace was no more.
Of Jesu Christ had they no dread
That they should do this evil deed?
'My gentle Bere of goode will!
He ne're did no man any ill.
He was sent to me of God's grace,
To be my help and my solace,
That God should send him me for love,
And they'd not suffer him to live.'

Almighty God shall do his will,
On them and all who did this ill.
Justice is And above the earth they soon were stinking
done That to the bere's death were consenting.

—— John Donne ——

[1572–1631]

From *Holy Sonnets*

'Why are we by all creatures waited on?'

Why are we by all creatures waited on?
 Why do the prodigal elements supply
Life and food to me, being more pure than I,
Simple, and further from corruption?
Why brook'st thou, ignorant horse, subjection?
Why dost thou, bull and boar, so seelily
Dissemble weakness, and by one man's stroke die
Whose whole kind you might swallow and feed upon?
Weaker I am, woe's me, and worse than you,
You have not sinn'd, nor need be timorous.

26

But wonder at a great wonder, for to us
Created nature doth these things subdue,
But their Creator, whom sin nor nature tied,
For us, his Creatures and his foes, hath died.

—— William Cartwright ——

[1611–1643]

The Dead Sparrow

Tell me not of joy; there's none,
　Now my little Sparrow's gone:
　　He, just as you,
　　Would try and woo,
He would chirp and flatter me;
He would hang the wing awhile –
Till at length he saw me smile.
Lord, how sullen he would be!

He would catch a crumb, and then
Sporting, let it go agen;
　　He from my lip
　　Would moisture sip;
He would from my trencher feed;
Then would hop, and then would run,
And cry Philip when he'd done.
O! whose heart can choose but bleed?

O how eager would he fight,
And ne'er hurt, though he did bite.
　　Nor morn did pass,
　　But on my glass
He would sit, and mark and do
What I did – now ruffle all
His feathers o'er, now let 'em fall;
And then straightway sleek them too.

Whence will Cupid get his darts
Feathered now to pierce our hearts?
 A wound he may
  Not, Love, convey,
Now this faithful bird is gone;
 O let mournful turtles join
 With loving red-breasts, and combine
To sing dirges o'er his stone!

—— Henry Vaughan ——

[1622–1695]

From *The Book*

Eternal God! Maker of all
 that have lived here, since the Man's fall;
the Rock of Ages! in whose shade
they live unseen, when here they fade.
Thou knew'st this paper, when it was
mere seed, and after that but grass;
before 'twas drest, or spun, and when
made linen, who did ear it then:
what were their lives, their thoughts and deeds
whether good corn, or fruitless weeds.
Thou knew'st this tree, when a green shade
cover'd it, since a cover made;
and where it flourished, grew, and spread,
as if it never should be dead.
Thou knew'st this harmless beast, when he
did live and feed by Thy decree
on each green thing; then slept (well-fed)
clothed with this skin, which now lies spread
a covering o'er this aged book,
which makes me wisely weep and look
on my own dust; here dust it is,

but not so dry and clean as this.
Thou knew'st and saw'st them all and though
now scatter'd thus, does know them so.
O knowing, glorious Spirit, when
Thou shalt restore trees, beasts and men,
when Thou shalt make all new again,
destroying only death and pain,
give him amongst Thy works a place,
who in them loved and sought Thy face.

──── Thomas Heyrick ────

[1649–1694]

On the Death of a Monkey

Here *Busy* and yet *Innocent* lyes Dead,
    two things, that seldom meet:
No plots nor Stratagems disturb'd his head,
    Or's his merry Soul did fret:
He shew'd like Superannuated *Peer*,
Grave was his look and *Politick* his Air;
And he for *Nothing* too spent all his care.

But that he died of Discontent, 'tis fear'd,
    Head of the *Monkey* Rout;
To see so many Brother *Apes* preferr'd,
    And he himself left out:
On all below he did his Anger show'r,
Fit for a Court did all above adore,
H'had *Shows* of Reason, and few *Men* have more.

29

John Gay

[1685–1732]

An Elegy on a Lap Dog

Shock's fate I mourn; poor *Shock* is now no more,
Ye Muses mourn, ye chamber-maids deplore.
Unhappy *Shock!* yet more unhappy Fair,
Doom's to survive thy joy and only care!
Thy wretched fingers now no more shall deck,
And tie the favourite ribbon round his neck;
Nomore thy hand shall smooth his glossy hair,
And comb the wavings of his pendent ear.
Yet cease thy flowing grief, forsaken maid;
All mortal pleasures in a moment fade:
Our surest hope is in an hour destroy'd,
And love, best gift of heav'n, not long enjoy'd.

Methinks I see her frantic with despair,
Her streaming eyes, wrung hands, and flowing hair;
Her *Mechlen* pinners rent the floor bestrow,
And her torn fan gives real signs of woe.
Hence Superstition, that tormenting guest,
That haunts with fancy'd fears the coward breast;
No dread events upon this fate attend,
Stream eyes no more, no more thy tresses rend.
Tho' certain omens oft forewarn a state,
And dying lions show the monarch's fate;
Why should such fears bid *Celia's* sorrow rise?
For when a Lap-dog falls, no lover dies.

Cease, *Celia*, cease; restrain thy flowing tears,
Some warmer passion will dispel thy cares.
In man you'll find a more substantial bliss,

More grateful toying, and a sweeter kiss.
He's dead. Oh lay him gently in the ground!
And may his tomb be by this verse renown'd.
Here Shock, *the pride of all his kind, is laid;*
Who fawn'd like man, but ne'er like man betray'd.

The Wild Boar and the Ram

Against an elm a sheep was ty'd;
the butcher's knife in blood was dy'd;
The patient flock, in silent fright,
From far beheld the horrid sight;
A savage Boar, who near them stood,
Thus mock'd to scorn the fleecy brood.

All cowards should be serv'd like you
See, see, your murd'rer is in view;
With purple hands and reeking knife
He strips the skin yet warm with life:
You quarter'd sires, your bleeding dams,
The dying beat of harmless lambs
Call for revenge. O stupid race!
The heart that wants revenge is base.

I grant, an ancient Ram replys,
We bear no terror in our eyes,
Yet think us not of soul so tame,
Which no repeated wrongs inflame;
Insensible of ev'ry ill,
Because we want thy tusks to kill.
Know, those who violence pursue
Give to themselves the vengeance due,
For in these massacres they find
The two chief plagues that waste mankind.
Our skin supplys the wrangling bar,
It wakes their slumbring sons to war,
And well revenge may rest contented,
Since drums and parchment were invented.

The Shepherd's Dog and the Wolf

A Wolf, with hunger fierce and bold,
ravaged the plains, and thinned the fold:
Deep in the wood secure he lay.
The thefts of night regaled the day.
In vain the shepherd's wakeful care,
Had spread the toils, and watched the snare;
In vain the Dog pursued his pace,
The fleeter robber mock'd the chase.

As Lightfoot ranged the forest round,
By chance his foe's retreat he found.
'Let us awhile the war suspend.
And reason as from friend to friend.'
'A truce?' replies the Wolf. 'Tis done.'
The Dog the parley thus begun:
'How can that strong intrepid mind
Attack a weak defenceless kind?

Those jaws should prey on nobler food,
And drink the boar's and lion's blood;
Great souls with generous pity melt,
Which coward tyrants never felt.
But harmless is our fleecy care!
Be brave, and let thy mercy spare.'
'Friend,' says the Wolf, 'the matter weigh;
Nature designed us beasts of prey;
As such, when hunger finds a treat,
'Tis necessary wolves should eat.
If, mindful of the bleating weal,
Thy bosom burn with real zeal;
Hence, and thy tyrant lord beseech;
To him repeat the moving speech:
A Wolf eats sheep but now and then,
Ten thousands are devoured by men.'
An open foe may prove a curse,
But pretended friend is worse.

Alexander Pope

[1688–1744]

From *Essay on Man*

Heav'n from all creatures hides the book of Fate,
all but the page prescrib'd, their present state:
From brutes what men, from men what spirits know:
Or who could suffer Being here below?
The lamb thy riot dooms to bleed today,
Had he thy Reason, would he skip and play?
Pleas'd to the last, he crops the flow'ry food,
And licks the hand just rais'd to shed his blood.

All are but parts of one stupendous whole,
Whose body Nature is, and God the soul . . .

Nor think, in Nature's State they blindly trod;
The state of Nature was the reign of God:
Self-love and Social at her birth began,
Union the bond of all things, and of Man.
Pride then was not; nor Arts, that Pride to aid;
Man walk'd with beast, joint tenant of the shade;
The same his table, and the same his bed;
No murder cloth'd him, and no murder fed.
In the same temple, the resounding wood,
All vocal beings hymn'd their equal God:
The shrine with gore unstain'd, with gold undrest,
Unbrib'd, unbloody, stood the blameless priest:
Heav'n's attribute was Universal Care,
And Man's prerogative to rule, but spare.
Ah! How unlike the man of times to come
Of half that live the butcher and the tomb;
Who, foe to Nature, hears the gen'ral groan,

Murders their species, and betrays his own.
But just disease to luxury succeeds,
And ev'ry death its own avenger breeds;
The Fury-passions from that blood began,
And turn'd on Man a fiercer savage, Man.

From *Windsor Forest*

See! from the brake the whirring pheasant springs,
  and mounts exulting on triumphant wings:
Short is his joy; he feels the fiery wound,
Flutters in blood, and panting beats the ground,
Ah! what avail his glossy, varying dyes,
His purple crest, and scarlet-circled eyes,
The vivid green his shining plumes unfold,
His painted wings, and breast that flames with gold?
  Nor yet, when moist Arcturus clouds the sky,
The woods and fields their pleasing toils deny.
To plains with well-breathed beagles we repair,
And trace the mazes of the circling hare:
(Beasts, urged by us, their fellow-beasts pursue,
And learn of man each other to undo).
With slaughtering guns th'unwearied fowler roves,
When frosts have whitened all the naked groves:
Where doves in flocks the leafless trees o'ershade,
And lonely woodcocks haunt the watery glade.
He lifts the tube, and levels with his eye;
Straight a short thunder breaks the frozen sky.
Oft, as in airy rings they skim the heath,
The clamorous lapwings feel the leaden death:
Oft, as the mounting larks their notes prepare,
They fall, and leave their little lives in air . . .

—— Oliver Goldsmith ——

[1728–1774]

An Elegy on the Death of a Mad Dog

Good people all, of every sort,
    give ear unto my song;
And if you find it wondrous short,
    It cannot hold you long.

In Islington there was a man,
    Of whom the world might say,
That still a godly race he ran,
    Whene're he went to pray.

A kind and gentle heart he had,
    To comfort friends and foes;
The naked every day he clad,
    When he put on his clothes.

And in that town a dog was found,
    As many dogs there be,
Both mongrel, puppy, whelp, and hound,
    And curs of low degree.

This dog and man at first were friends;
    But when a pique began,
The dog, to gain some private ends,
    Went mad, and bit the man.

Around from all the neighbouring streets,
    The wondering neighbours ran,
And swore the dog has lost his wits,
    To bite so good a man.

The wound it seemed both sore and sad
   To every Christian eye;
And while they swore the dog was mad,
   They swore the man would die.

But soon a wonder came to light,
   That showed the rogues they lied;
The man recovered of the bite,
   The dog it was that died.

The Hermit

Then turn to-night, and freely share
   whate'er my cell bestows,
My rushy couch and frugal fare,
   My blessing and repose.

No flocks that range the valley free,
   To slaughter I condemn;
Taught by the power that pities me,
   I learn to pity them.

But from the mountain's grassy side,
   A guiltless feast I bring,
A scrip with herbs and fruit supplied,
   And water from the spring.

Then, pilgrim, turn, thy cares forego,
   All earth-born cares are wrong;
Man wants but little here below,
   Nor wants that little long.

William Cowper

[1731–1800]

The Nightingale and the Glow-Worm

A Nightingale, that all day long
  had cheer'd the village with his song,
Nor yet at eve his note suspended,
Nor yet when eventide was ended,
Began to feel, as well he might,
The keen demands of appetite;
When, looking eagerly around,
He spied far off upon the ground,
A something shining in the dark,
And knew the glow-worm by his spark.
So stooping down from hawthorn top,
He thought to put him in his crop:
The worm, aware of his intent,
Harangued him thus right eloquent.
  Did you admire my lamp, quoth he,
As much as I your minstrelsy,
You should abhor to do me wrong,
As much as I to spoil your song;
For 'twas the self-same Pow'r divine,
Taught you to sing, and me to shine;
That you with music, I with light,
Might beautify and cheer the night.
The songster heard his short oration,
And warbling out his approbation,
Released him as my story tells,
And found a supper somewhere else.
  Hence jarring sectaries may learn
Their real interest to discern:
That brother should not war with brother,

37

And worry and devour each other;
But sing and shine by sweet consent,
Till life's poor transient night is spent,
Respecting in each other's case
The gifts of nature and of grace.
   Those Christians best deserve the name
Who studiously make peace their aim;
Peace, both the duty and the prize
Of him that creeps and him that flies.

On a Goldfinch Starved to Death in a Cage

Time was when I was free as air,
   the thistle's downy seed my fare,
   My drink the morning dew:
I perch'd at will on ev'ry spray,
My form genteel, my plumage gay,
   My strains for ever new.

But gaudy plumage, sprightly strain,
And form genteel were all in vain
   And of a transient date;
For caught and caged and starved to death,
In dying sighs my little breath
   Soon pass'd the wiry grate.

Thanks, gentle swain, for all my woes,
And thanks for this effectual close
   And cure of ev'ry ill!
More cruelty could none express,
And I, if you had shown me less,
   Had been your pris'ner still.

From *The Garden*

Oh, friendly to the best pursuits of man,
   Friendly to thought, to virtue, and to peace,
Domestic life in rural leisure pass'd!
Few know thy value, and few taste thy sweets,

Though many boast thy favours, and affect
To understand and choose thee for their own.
But foolish man foregoes his proper bliss,
Ev'n as his first progenitor, and quits,
Though placed in paradise (for each has still
Some traces of her youthful beauty left),
Substantial happiness for transient joy.
Scenes form'd for contemplation, and to nurse
The growing seeds of wisdom; that suggest,
By ev'ry pleasing image they present,
Reflections such as meliorate the heart,
Compose the passions, and exalt the mind;
Scenes such as these, 'tis his supreme delight
To fill with riot and defile with blood.
Should some contagion, kind to the poor brutes
We persecute, annihilate the tribes
That draw the sportsman over hill and dale
Fearless, and rapt away from all his cares;
Should never game-fowl hatch her eggs again,
Nor baited hook deceive the fish's eye;
Could pageantry, and dance, and feast, and song
Be quell'd in all our summer-months' retreats;
How many self-deluded nymphs and swains,
Who dream they have a taste for fields and groves
Would find them hideous nurs'ries of the spleen,
And crowd the roads, impatient for the town!
They love the country, and none else, who seek
For their own sake its silence and its shade;
Delights which who would leave, that has a heart
Susceptible of pity, or a mind
Cultured and capable of sober thought,
For all the savage din of the swift pack,
And clamours of the field? Detested sport,
That owes its pleasures to another's pain,
That feeds upon the sobs and dying shrieks
Of harmless nature, dumb, but yet endued
With eloquence, that agonies inspire,
Of silent tears and heart-distending sighs!
Vain tears, alas! and sighs that never find
A corresponding tone in jovial souls.
Well – one at least is safe. One shelter'd hare
Has never heard the sanguinary yell

Of cruel men, exulting in her woes.
Innocent partner of my peaceful home,
Whom ten long years' experience of my care
Has made at last familiar, she has lost
Most of her vigilant instinctive dread,
Not needful here, beneath a roof like mine.
Yes – thou mayst eat thy bread, and lick the hand
That feeds thee; thou mayst frolic on the floor
At evening, and at night retire secure
To thy straw-couch, and slumber unalarm'd;
For I have gain'd thy confidence, have pledged
All that is human in me, to protect
Thine unsuspecting gratitude and love.
If I survive thee I will dig thy grave,
And when I place thee in it, sighing say,
I knew at least one hare that had a friend.

The Cockfighter's Garland[1]

Muse — Hide his name of whom I sing,
   lest his surviving house thou bring
  For his sake into scorn,
Nor speak the school from which he drew
The much or little that he knew,
  Nor place where he was born.

That such a man once was, may seem
Worthy of record (if the theme
  Perchance may credit win)
For proof to man, what man may prove,
If grace depart, and demons move
  The source of guilt within.

This man (for since the howling wild
Disclaims him, man he must be styled)
  Wanted no good below;

---

[1] 'I have composed a small poem on a hideous subject, with which the "Gentleman's Magazine" for April furnished me: it is, nevertheless, a true one, hideous as it is. Mr. Bull and Mr. Greathead, who both have seen the man on whose death it is written, know that he died as there related' (June 6, 1789).

Gentle he was, if gentle birth
Could make him such, and he had worth,
  If wealth could worth bestow.

In social talk and ready jest,
He shone superior at the feast,
  And qualities of mind,
Illustrious in the eyes of those,
Whose gay society he chose,
  Possess'd of ev'ry kind.

Methinks I see him powder'd red,
With bushy locks his well-dress'd head
  Wing'd broad on either side.
The mossy rose-bud not so sweet;
His steeds superb, his carriage neat
  As lux'ry could provide.

Can such be cruel? Such can be
Cruel as hell, and so was he;
  A tyrant entertain'd
With barb'rous sports, whose fell delight
Was to encourage mortal fight
  'Twixt birds to battle train'd.

One feather'd champion he possess'd,
His darling far beyond the rest,
  Which never knew disgrace,
Nor e'er had fought, but he made flow
The life-blood of his fiercest foe,
  The Caesar of his race.

It chanced, at last, when, on a day,
He push'd him to the desp'rate fray,
  His courage droop'd, he fled.
The master storm'd, the prize was lost,
And, instant, frantic at the cost,
  He doom'd his fav'rite dead.

He seiz'd him fast, and from the pit
Flew to the kitchen, snatch'd the spit,
  And, bring me cord, he cried;

41

The cord was brought, and, at his word,
To that dire implement the bird
    Alive and struggling tied.

The horrid sequel asks a veil,
And all the terrors of the tale
    That can be, shall be, sunk –
Led by the suff'rer's screams aright,
his shock'd companions view the sight
    And him with fury drunk.

All, suppliant, beg a milder fate
For the old warrior at the grate:
    He deaf to pity's call
Whirl'd round him rapid as a wheel
His culinary club of steel,
    Death menacing on all.

But vengeance hung not far remote,
For while he stretch'd his clam'rous throat,
    And heav'n and earth defied,
Big with a curse too closely pent
That struggled vainly for a vent,
    He totter'd, reel'd, and died.

'Tis not for us, with rash surmise,
To point the judgments of the skies,
    But judgments plain as this,
That, sent for man's instruction, bring
A written label on their wing,
    'Tis hard to read amiss.

Epigram

To purify their wine, some people bleed
    a lamb into the barrel, and succeed;
No nostrum, planters say, is half so good
To make fine sugar, as a negro's blood.
Now lambs and negroes both are harmless things,
And hence perhaps the wondrous virtue springs.

'Tis in the blood of innocence alone —
Good cause why planters never try their own.

Epitaph on Fop,
A Dog Belonging to Lady Throckmorton

Though once a puppy, and though Fop by name
　Here moulders one whose bones some honour claim
No sycophant, although of spaniel race,
And though no hound, a martyr to the chase –
Ye squirrels, rabbits, leverets, rejoice,
Your haunts no longer echo to his voice;
This record of his fate exulting view,
He died worn out with vain pursuit of you.

'Yes' – the indignant shade of Fop replies –
'And worn with vain pursuit Man also dies.'

From *The Winter Walk at Noon*

Man scarce had risen, obedient to His call
　who form'd him from the dust, his future grave,
When he was crown'd as never king was since.
God set the diadem upon his head,
And angel choirs attended. Wond'ring stood
The new-made monarch, while before him pass'd,
All happy and all perfect in their kind,
The creatures, summon'd from their various haunts
To see their sov'reign, and confess his sway.
Vast was his empire, absolute his pow'r,
Or bounded only by a law whose force
'Twas his sublimest privilege to feel
And own, the law of universal love.
He ruled with meekness, they obey'd with joy.
And no distrust of his intent in theirs.
So Eden was a scene of harmless sport,
Where kindness on his part who ruled the whole
Begat a tranquil confidence in all,
And fear as yet was not, nor cause for fear.
But sin marr'd all; and the revolt of man,

That source of evils not exhausted yet,
Was punish'd with revolt of his from him.
Garden of God, how terrible the change
Thy groves and lawns then witness'd! ev'ry heart,
Each animal of ev'ry name, conceived
A jealousy and an instinctive fear,
And, conscious of some danger, either fled
Precipitate the loathed abode of man,
Or growl'd defiance in such angry sort,
As taught him too to tremble in his turn.
Thus harmony and family accord
Were driv'n from Paradise; and in that hour
The seeds of cruelty, that since have swell'd
To such gigantic and enormous growth,
Were sown in human nature's fruitful soil.
Hence date the persecution and the pain
That man inflicts on all inferior kinds,
Regardless of their plaints. To make him sport,
To gratify the frenzy of his wrath,
Or his base gluttony, are causes good
And just, in his account, why bird and beast
Should suffer torture, and the streams be dyed
With blood of their inhabitants impaled.
Earth groans beneath the burden of a war
Waged with defenceless innocence, while he,
Not satisfied to prey on all around,
Adds tenfold bitterness to death by pangs
Needless, and first torments ere he devours.
Now happiest they that occupy the scenes
The most remote from his abhorr'd resort,
Whom once as delegate of God on earth
They fear'd, and as his perfect image loved.
The wilderness is theirs with all its caves,
Its hollow glens, its thickets, and its plains
Unvisited by man. There they are free,
And howl and roar as likes them, uncontroll'd,
Nor ask his leave to slumber or to play.
Woe to the tyrant, if he dare intrude
Within the confines of their wild domain;
The lion tells him — I am monarch here —
And if he spares him, spares him on the terms
Of royal mercy, and through gen'rous scorn

To rend a victim trembling at his foot.
In measure, as by force of instinct drawn,
Or by necessity constrain'd, they live
Dependent upon man, those in his fields,
These at his crib, and some beneath his roof,
They prove too often at how dear a rate
He sells protection. Witness, at his foot
The spaniel dying for some venial fault,
Under dissection of the knotted scourge;
Witness, the patient ox, with stripes and yells
Driven to the slaughter, goaded as he runs
To madness, while the savage at his heels
Laughs at the frantic suff'rer's fury spent
Upon the guiltless passenger o'erthrown.
He too is witness, noblest of the train
That wait on man, the flight-performing horse:
With unsuspecting readiness he takes
His murd'rer on his back, and, push'd all day,
With bleeding sides, and flanks that heave for life,
To the far-distant goal, arrives and dies.
So little mercy shows who need so much!
Does law, so jealous of the cause of man,
Denounce no doom on the delinquent? None.
He lives, and o'er his brimming beaker boasts
(As if barbarity were high desert)
Th'inglorious feat, and, clamorous in praise
Of the poor brute, seems wisely to suppose
The honours of his matchless horse his own.
But many a crime, deem'd innocent on earth,
Is register'd in heav'n, and these, no doubt,
Have each their record, with a curse annex'd.
Man may dismiss compassion from his heart,
But God will never. When he charged the Jew
T'assist his foe's down-fallen beast to rise,
And when the bush-exploring boy that seized
The young, to let the parent bird go free,
Proved he not plainly that his meaner works
Are yet his care, and have an interest all,
All, in the universal Father's love.
On Noah, and in him on all mankind,
The charter was conferr'd by which we hold
The flesh of animals in fee, and claim,

O'er all we feed on, power of life and death.
But read the instrument, and mark it well;
Th'oppression of a tyrannous control
Can find no warrant there. Feed then, and yield
Thanks for thy food. Carnivorous, through sin,
Feed on the slain, but spare the living brute.

The Governor of all, himself to all
So bountiful, in whose attentive ear
The unfledged raven and the lion's whelp
Plead not in vain for pity on the pangs
Of hunger unassuaged, has interposed,
Not seldom, his avenging arm, to smite
Th'injurious trampler upon nature's law,
That claims forbearance even for a brute.
He hates the hardness of a Balaam's heart;
And, prophet as he was, he might not strike
The blameless animal, without rebuke,
On which he rode. Her opportune offence
Saved him, or th'unrelenting seer had died.
He sees that human equity is slack
To interfere, though in so just a cause,
And makes the task his own; inspiring dumb
And helpless victims with a sense so keen
Of injury, with such knowledge of their strength,
And such sagacity to take revenge,
That oft the beast has seem'd to judge the man.
An ancient, not a legendary tale,
By one of sound intelligence rehearsed,
(If such, who plead for Providence, may seem
In modern eyes) shall make the doctrine clear . . .

I would not enter on my list of friends
(Though graced with polish'd manners and fine sense
Yet wanting sensibility) the man
Who needlessly sets foot upon a worm.
An inadvertent step may crush the snail
That crawls at evening in the public path;
But he that has humanity, forewarn'd,
Will tread aside, and let the reptile live.
The creeping vermin, loathsome to the sight,
And charged perhaps with venom, that intrudes

A visitor unwelcome into scenes
Sacred to neatness and repose, th'alcove,
The chamber, or refectory, may die.
A necessary act incurs no blame.
Not so when, held within their proper bounds
And guiltless of offence, they range the air,
Or take their pastime in the spacious field.
There they are privileged; and he that hunts
Or harms them there is guilty of a wrong,
Disturbs th'economy of nature's realm,
Who, when she form'd, design'd them an abode.
The sum is this: if man's convenience, health,
Or safety interfere, his rights and claims
Are paramount, and must extinguish theirs.
Else they are all — the meanest things that are,
As free to live and to enjoy that life,
As God was free to form them at the first,
Who in his sov'reign wisdom made them all.
Ye, therefore, who love mercy, teach your sons
To love it too. The spring-time of our years
Is soon dishonour'd and defiled in most
By budding ills, that ask a prudent hand
To check them. But, alas! none sooner shoots,
If unrestrain'd, into luxuriant growth,
Than cruelty, most dev'lish of them all.
Mercy to him that shows it, is the rule
And righteous limitation of its act,
By which Heav'n moves in pard'ning guilty man;
And he that shows none, being ripe in years,
And conscious of the outrage he commits,
Shall seek it, and not find it in his turn.

   Distinguish'd much by reason, and still more
By our capacity of grace divine,
From creatures that exist but for our sake,
Which having served us, perish, we are held
Accountable, and God, some future day,
Will reckon with us roundly for th'abuse
Of what he deems no mean or trivial trust.
Superior as we are, they yet depend
Not more on human help, than we on theirs.
Their strength, or speed, or vigilance, were giv'n

In aid of our defects. In some are found
Such teachable and apprehensive parts,
That man's attainments in his own concerns,
Match'd with th'expertness of the brutes in theirs,
Are oft times vanquish'd and thrown far behind.
Some show that nice sagacity of smell,
And read with such discernment, in the port
And figure of the man, his secret aim,
That oft we owe our safety to a skill
We could not teach, and must despair to learn.
But learn we might, if not too proud to stoop
To quadruped instructors, many a good
And useful quality, and virtue too,
Rarely exemplified among ourselves;
Attachment never to be weaned, or changed
By any change of fortune, proof alike
Against unkindness, absence, and neglect;
Fidelity, that neither bribe nor threat
Can move or warp; and gratitude for small
And trivial favours, lasting as the life,
And glist'ning even in the dying eye . . .
And I, contented with a humble theme,
Have pour'd my stream of panegyric down
The vale of nature, where it creeps and winds
Among her lovely works, with a secure
And unambitious course, reflecting clear
If not the virtues yet the worth of brutes.
And I am recompensed, and deem the toils
Of poetry not list, if verse of mine
May stand between an animal and woe,
And teach one tyrant pity for his drudge.

The groans of nature in this nether world,
Which Heav'n has heard for ages, have an end.
Foretold by prophets, and by poets sung,
Whose fire was kindled at the prophets' lamp,
The time of rest, the promised sabbath, comes.
Six thousand years of sorrow have well-nigh
Fulfill'd their tardy and disastrous course
Over a sinful world; and what remains
Of this tempestuous state of human things,
Is merely as the working of a sea

Before a calm, that rocks itself to rest.
For He, whose care the winds are, and the clouds
The dust that waits upon his sultry march,
When sin hath moved him, and his wrath is hot,
Shall visit earth in mercy; shall descend
Propitious, in his chariot paved with love,
And what his storms have blasted and defaced
For man's revolt, shall with a smile repair.

Sweet is the harp of prophecy; too sweet
Not to be wrong'd by a mere mortal touch;
Nor can the wonders it records be sung
To meaner music, and not suffer loss.
But when a poet, or when one like me,
Happy to rove among poetic flow'rs,
Though poor in skill to rear them, lights at last
On some fair theme, some theme divinely fair,
Such is the impulse and the spur he feels
To give it praise proportion'd to its worth,
That not t'attempt it, arduous as he deems
The labour, were a task more arduous still.

Oh scenes surpassing fable, and yet true,
Scenes of accomplish'd bliss! which who can see,
Though but in distant prospect, and not feel
His soul refresh'd with foretaste of the joy?
Rivers of gladness water all the earth,
And clothe all climes with beauty; the reproach
Of barrenness is past. The fruitful field
Laughs with abundance, and the land once lean,
Or fertile only in its own disgrace,
Exults to see its thistly curse repeal'd.
The various seasons woven into one,
And that one season an eternal spring,
The garden fears no blight, and needs no fence,
For there is none to covet, all are full.
The lion and the libbard and the bear
Graze with the fearless flocks. All bask at noon
Together, or all gambol in the shade
Of the same grove, and drink one common stream.
Antipathies are none. No foe to man
Lurks in the serpent now. The mother sees,

And smiles to see, her infant's playful hand
Stretch'd forth to dally with the crested worm.
To stroke his azure neck, or to receive
The lambent homage of his arrowy tongue.
All creatures worship man, and all mankind
One Lord, one Father. Error has no place;
That creeping pestilence is driven away,
The breath of heav'n has chased it. In the heart
No passion touches a discordant string,
But all is harmony and love. Disease
Is not. The pure and uncontaminate blood
Holds its due course, nor fears the frost of age.
One song employs all nations; and all cry,
'Worthy the Lamb, for he was slain for us!'
The dwellers in the vales and on the rocks
Shout to each other, and the mountain tops
From distant mountains catch the flying joy,
Till nation after nation taught the strain,
Each rolls the rapturous Hosanna round.
Behold the measure of the promise fill'd,
See Salem built, the labour of a God!
Bright as a sun the sacred city shines;
All kingdoms and all princes of the earth
Flock to that light; the glory of all lands
Flows into her, unbounded is her joy
And endless her increase. Thy rams are there
Nebaioth, and the flocks of Kedar there;
The looms of Ormus, and the mines of Ind,
And Saba's spicy groves pay tribute there.
Praise is in all her gates. Upon her walls,
And in her streets, and in her spacious courts
Is heard salvation. Eastern Java there
Kneels with the native of the farthest West,
And Æthiopia spreads abroad the hand,
and worships. Her report has travell'd forth
Into all lands. From every clime they come
To see thy beauty and to share thy joy,
O Sion! an assembly such as earth
Saw never; such as heav'n stoops down to see.

   Thus heav'nward all things tend. For all were once
Perfect, and all must be at length restored.

So God has greatly purposed; who would else
In his dishonour'd works himself endure
Dishonour, and be wrong'd without redress.

—— William Blake ——

[1757–1827]

Auguries of Innocence

To see a World in a Grain of Sand
    and a Heaven in a Wild Flower,
Hold Infinity in the palm of your hand
And Eternity in an hour.
A Robin Red breast in a Cage
Puts all Heaven in a Rage.
A Dove house fill'd with Doves & Pigeons
Shudders Hell thro' all its regions.
A Dog stav'd at his Master's Gate
Predicts the ruin of the State.
A Horse misus'd upon the Road
Calls to Heaven for human blood.
Each outcry of the hunted Hare
A fibre from the Brain does tear.
A Skylark wounded in the wing,
A Cherubim does cease to sing.
The Game Cock clip'd & arm'd for fight
Does the Rising Sun affright.
Every Wolf's & Lion's howl
Raises from Hell a Human Soul.
The wild Deer wand'ring here & there
Keeps the Human Soul from Care.
The Lamb misus'd breeds Public strife
And yet forgives the Butcher's Knife.
The Bat that flits at close of Eve
Has left the Brain that won't Believe.

The Owl that calls upon the Night
Speaks the Unbeliever's fright.
He who shall hurt the little Wren
Shall never be belov'd by Men.
He who the Ox to wrath has mov'd
Shall never be by Woman lov'd.
The wanton Boy that kills the Fly
Shall feel the Spider's enmity.
He who torments the Chafer's sprite
Weaves a Bower in endless Night.
The Catterpiller on the Leaf
Repeats to thee thy Mother's grief.
Kill not the Moth nor Butterfly
For the Last Judgment draweth nigh.
He who shall train the Horse to war
Shall never pass the Polar Bar.
The Beggar's Dog & Widow's Cat,
Feed them, & thou wilt grow fat.
The Gnat that sings his Summer's song
Poison gets from Slander's tongue.
The poison of the Snake & Newt
Is the sweat of Envy's Foot.
The Poison of the Honey Bee
Is the Artist's Jealousy.
The Prince's Robes & Beggar's Rags
Are Toadstools on the Miser's Bags.
A truth that's told with bad intent
Beats all the Lies you can invent.
It is right it should be so;
Man was made for Joy & Woe,
And when this we rightly know
Thro' the World we safely go.
Joy & Woe are woven fine,
A Clothing for the Soul divine;
Under every grief & pine
Runs a joy with silken twine.
The Babe is more than swadling Bands;
Throughout all these Human Lands
Tools were made, & Born were hands,
Every Farmer Understands.
Every Tear from Every Eye
Becomes a Babe in Eternity;

This is caught by Females bright
And return'd to its own delight.
The Bleat, the Bark, Bellow & Roar
Are Waves that Beat on Heaven's Shore.
The Babe that weeps the Rod beneath
Writes Revenge in realms of Death.
The Beggar's Rags, fluttering in Air,
Does to Rags the Heavens tear.
The Soldier arm'd with Sword & Gun
Palsied strikes the Summer's Sun.
The poor Man's Farthing is worth more
Than all the Gold on Afric's Shore.
One Mite wrung from the Lab'rer's hands
Shall buy & sell the Miser's Lands:
Or, if protected from on high,
Does that whole Nation sell & buy.
He who mocks the Infant's Faith
Shall be mock'd in Age & Death.
He who shall teach the Child to Doubt
The rotting Grave shall ne'er get out.
He who respects the Infant's faith
Triumphs over Hell & Death.
The Child's Toys & the Old Man's Reasons
Are the Fruits of the Two seasons.
The Questioner who sits so sly
Shall never know how to Reply.
He who replies to words of Doubt
Doth put the Light of Knowledge out.
The Strongest Poison ever known
Came from Caesar's Laurel Crown.
Nought can deform the Human Race
Like to the Armour's iron brace.
When Gold & Gems adorn the Plow
To peaceful Arts shall Envy Bow.
A Riddle or the Cricket's Cry
Is to Doubt a fit Reply.
The Emmet's Inch & Eagle's Mile
Make Lame Philosophy to smile.
He who Doubts from what he sees
Will ne'er Believe, do what you Please.
If the Sun & Moon should doubt,
They'd immediately Go out.

To be in a Passion you Good may do,
But no Good if a Passion is in you.
The Whore & Gambler, by the State
Licenc'd, build that Nation's Fate.
The Harlot's cry from Street to Street
Shall weave Old England's winding Sheet.
The Winner's Shout, the Loser's Curse,
Dance before dead England's Hearse.
Every Night & every Morn
Some to Misery are Born.
Every Morn & every Night
Some are Born to sweet delight.
Some are Born to Endless Night.
We are led to Believe a Lie
When we see not Thro' the Eye
Which was Born in a Night, to perish in a Night,
When the Soul Slept in Beams of Light.
To those poor Souls who dwell in Night,
But does Human Form Display
To those who Dwell in Realms of Day.

The Tiger

Tiger, tiger, burning bright
  in the forests of the night,
What immortal hand or eye
Could frame thy fearful symmetry?

In what distant deeps or skies
Burnt the fire of thine eyes?
On what wings dare he aspire?
What the hand dare seize the fire?

And what shoulder and what art
Could twist the sinews of thy heart?
And when thy heart began to beat,
What dread hand? And what dread feet?

What the hammer? What the chain?
In what furnace was thy brain?
What the anvil? What dread grasp
Dare its deadly terrors clasp?

When the stars threw down their spears
And watered Heaven with their tears,
Did he smile his work to see?
Did he who made the Lamb make thee?

Tiger, tiger, burning bright
In the forests of the night,
What immortal hand or eye
Dare frame thy fearful symmetry?

The Lamb

Little Lamb, who made thee?
   Dost thou know who made thee?
Gave thee life and bid thee feed
By the stream and o'er the mead;
Gave thee clothing of delight,
Softest clothing, woolly, bright;
Gave thee such a tender voice
Making all the vales rejoice?
  Little Lamb who made thee?
  Dost thou know who made thee?

  Little Lamb, I'll tell thee,
  Little Lamb, I'll tell thee:
He is callèd by thy name,
For he calls himself a Lamb.
He is meek and he is mild;
He became a little child.
I a child and thou a lamb,
We are called by his name.

Little Lamb, God bless thee.
Little Lamb, God bless thee.

Robert Burns

(1759–1796)

On Scaring some Waterfowl in Loch-Turit,
A Wild Scene amid the Hills of Oughtertyre

Why, ye tenants of the lake,
   for me your watery haunt forsake?
Tell me, fellow-creatures, why
At my presence thus you fly?
Why disturb your social joys,
Parent, filial, kindred ties?
Common friend to you and me,
Nature's gifts to all are free:
Peaceful keep your dimpling wave,
Busy feed, or wanton lave;
Or, beneath the sheltering rock,
Bide the surging billow's shock.

Conscious, blushing for our race,
Soon, too soon, your fears I trace.
Man, your proud usurping foe,
Would be lord of all below;
Plumes himself in Freedom's pride,
Tyrant stern to all beside.

The eagle, from the cliffy brow,
Marking you his prey below,
In his breast no pity dwells,
Strong necessity compels.
But man, to whom alone is given
A ray direct from pitying Heaven,
Glories in his heart humane –
And creatures for his pleasure slain.

In these savage, liquid plains,
Only known to wand'ring swains,
Where the mossy riv'let strays;
Far from human haunts and ways;
All on Nature you depend,
And life's poor season peaceful spend.

Or, if man's superior might,
Dare invade your native right,
On the lofty ether borne,
Man with all his powers you scorn;
Swiftly seek, on clanging wings,
Other lakes and other springs;
And the foe you cannot brave,
Scorn at least to be his slave.

To a Mouse

Wee, sleekit, cowrin', tim'rous beastie,
    Oh, what a panic's in thy breastie!
Thou needna start awa'sae hasty,
    Wi' bick'ring brattle!
I wad be laith to rin and chase thee,
    Wi' murd'ring pattle!
I'm truly sorry man's dominion
Has broken nature's social union,
and justifies that ill opinion
    Which mak's thee startle
At me, thy poor earth-born companion,
    And fellow-mortal!

I doubt na, whyles, but thou may thieve;
What then? poor beastie, thou maun live
A daimen icker in a thrave
    'S a sma'request:
I'll get a blessin' wi' the lave,
    And never miss't.

Thy wee bit housie, too, in ruin!
It's silly wa's the win's are strewin'!
And naething now to big a new ane
   O' foggage green!
And bleak December's winds ensuin',
   Baith snell and keen!

Thou saw the fields laid bare and waste,
And weary winter comin' fast,
And cozie here, beneath the blast
   Thou thought to dwell,
Till, crash! the cruel coulter past
   Out through thy cell.

That wee bit heap o' leaves and stibble
Has cost thee mony a weary nibble!
Now thou's turned out for a' thy trouble,
   But house or hauld,
To thole the winter's sletty dribble,
   And cranreuch cauld!

But, Mousie, thou art no thy lane
In proving foresight maybe vain!
The best-laid schemes o' mice and men
   Gang aft a-gley,
And lea'e us nought but grief and pain
   For promised joy.

Still thou art blest, compared wi' me!
The present only toucheth thee:
But, och! I backward cast my e'e
   On prospects drear!
And forward, though I canna see,
   I guess and fear.

On Seeing a Wounded Hare Limp by Me which a Fellow had Just Shot At

Inhuman man! curse on thy barb'rous art,
   And blasted be thy murder-aiming eye:
May never pity soothe thee with a sigh,
Nor ever pleasure glad thy cruel heart!

Go live, poor wanderer of the wood and field
The bitter little that of life remains:
No more the thickening brakes and verdant plains
To thee shall home, or food, or pastime yield.

Seek, mangled wretch, some place of wonted rest
No more of rest, but now thy dying bed!
The sheltering rushes whistling o'er thy head,
The cold earth with thy bloody bosom prest.

Oft as by winding Nith I, musing, wait
The sober eve, or hail the cheerful dawn,
I'll miss thee sporting o'er the dewy lawn,
And curse the ruffian's aim, and mourn thy hapless fate.

——— Robert Bloomfield ———

[1766–1823]

From *Winter*

The Ploughman's Horse

Sweet then the ploughman's slumbers, hale and young,
When the last topic dies upon his tongue;
Sweet then the bliss his transient dreams inspire,
Till chilblains wake him, or the snapping fire.
  He starts, and ever thoughtful of his team,
Along the glittering snow a feeble gleam
Shoots from his lantern, as he yawning goes
To add fresh comforts to their night's repose;
Diffusing fragrance as their food he moves,
And pats the jolly sides of those he loves.
Thus full replenished, perfect ease possessed,
From night till morn alternate food and rest,
No rightful cheer witheld, no sleep debarred,

Their each day's labour brings its sure reward.
Yet when from plough or lumbering cart set free,
They taste awhile the sweets of liberty:
E'en sober Dobbin lifts his clumsy heel
And kicks, disdainful of the dirty wheel;
But soon, his frolic ended, yields again
To trudge the road, and wear the clinking chain.
   Short-sighted Dobbin! . . . thou canst only see
The trivial hardships that encompass thee:
Thy chains were freedom, and thy toils repose,
Could the poor post-horse tell thee all his woes;
Show thee his bleeding shoulders, and unfold
The dreadful anguish he endures for gold:
Hired at each call of business, lust, or rage,
That prompts the traveller on from stage to stage,
Still on his strength depends their boasted speed;
From them his limbs grow weak, his bare ribs bleed;
And though he groaning quickens at command,
Their extra shilling in the rider's hand
Becomes his bitter scourge; . . . 'tis he must feel
The double efforts of the lash and steel;
Till when, up hill, the destined inn he gains,
And trembling under complicated pains,
Prone from his nostrils, darting on the ground,
His breath emitted floats in clouds around,
Drops chase each other down his chest and dies,
And spattered mud his native colour hides:
Through his swoln veins the boiling torrent flows,
And every nerve a separate torture knows.
His harness loosed, he welcomes eager-eyed
The pail's full draught that quivers by his side;
And joys to see the well-known stable door,
As the starved mariner the friendly shore.
   Ah, well for him if here his sufferings ceased,
And ample hours of rest his pains appeased!
But roused again, and sternly bade to rise,
And shake refreshing slumber from his eyes,
Ere his exhausted spirits can return,
Or through his frame reviving ardour burn,
Come forth he must, though limping, maimed, and sore;
He hears the whip; the chaise is at the door: . . .
The collar tightens, and again he feels

His half-healed wounds inflamed; again the wheels
With tiresome sameness in his ears resound,
O'er blinding dust, or miles of flinty ground.
Thus nightly robbed, and injured day by day,
His piece-meal murderers wear his life away.

—— William Wordsworth ——

[1770–1850]

From *Lines*
Composed a few miles above Tintern Abbey,
on Revisiting the Banks of the Wye during a Tour,
July 13, 1798

For I have learned
to look on nature, not as in the hour
Of thoughtless youth; but hearing oftentimes
The still, sad music of humanity,
Nor harsh nor grating, though of ample power
To chasten and subdue. And I have felt
A presence that disturbs me with the joy
Of elevated thoughts; a sense sublime
Of something far more deeply interfused,
Whose dwelling is the light of setting suns,
And the round ocean and the living air,
And the blue sky, and in the mind of man:
A motion and a spirit, that impels
All thinking things, all objects of all thought,
And rolls through all things. Therefore am I still
A lover of the meadows and the woods,
And mountains; and of all that we behold
From this green earth; of all the mighty world
Of eye, and ear, — both what they half create,
And what perceive; well pleased to recognise
In nature and the language of the sense

The anchor of my purest thoughts, the nurse,
The guide, the guardian of my heart, and soul
Of all my moral being.
   Nor perchance,
If I were not thus taught, should I the more
Suffer my genial spirits to decay:
For thou art with me here upon the banks
Of this fair river; thou my dearest Friend,
My dear, dear Friend; and in thy voice I catch
The language of my former heart, and read
My former pleasures in the shooting lights
Of thy wild eyes. Oh! yet a little while
May I behold in thee what I was once,
My dear, dear Sister! and this prayer I make,
Knowing that Nature never did betray
The heart that loved her; 'tis her privilege,
Through all the years of this our life, to lead
From joy to joy: for she can so inform
The mind that is within us, so impress
With quietness and beauty, and so feed
With lofty thoughts, that neither evil tongues,
Rash judgments, nor the sneers of selfish men,
Nor greetings where no kindness is, nor all
The dreary intercourse of daily life,
Shall e'er prevail against us, or disturb
Our cheerful faith, that all which we behold
Is full of blessings. Therefore let the moon
Shine on thee in thy solitary walk;
And let the misty mountain-winds be free
To blow against thee: and, in after years,
When these wild ecstasies shall be matured
Into a sober pleasure; when thy mind
Shall be a mansion for all lovely forms,
Thy memory be as a dwelling-place
For all sweet sounds and harmonies; oh! then
If solitude, or fear, or pain, or grief,
Should be thy portion, with what healing thoughts
Of tender joy wilt thou remember me,
And these my exhortations! Nor, perchance —
If I should be where I no more can hear
Thy voice, nor catch from thy wild eyes these gleams
Of past existence — wilt thou then forget

That on the banks of this delightful stream
We stood together; and that I, so long
A worshipper of Nature, hither came
Unwearied in that service: rather say
with warmer love — oh! with far deeper zeal
Of holier love. Nor wilt thou then forget
That after many wanderings, many years
Of absence, these steep woods and lofty cliffs,
And this green pastoral landscape, were to me
More dear, both for themselves and for thy sake!

To a Skylark

Ethereal minstrel! pilgrim of the sky!
Dost thou despise the earth where cares
abound?
Or, while the wings aspire, the heart and eye
Both with thy nest upon the dewy ground?
The nest which thou canst drop into at will,
Those quivering wings composed, that music still!

Leave to the nightingale her shady wood;
A privacy of glorious light is thine;
Whence thou dost pour upon the world a flood
Of harmony, with instinct more divine;
Type of the wise who soar, but never roam;
True to the kindred points of Heaven and Home!

From *The Cuckoo at Laverna*
(on St Francis of Assisi)

Out of the cleansed heart
Of that once sinful Being overflowed
On sun, moon, stars, the nether elements,
And every shape of creature they sustain,
Divine affections; and with beast and bird
(Stilled from afar — such marvel story tells —
By casual outbreak of his passionate words,
And from their own pursuits in field and grove
Drawn to his side by look or act of love

Humane, and virtue of his innocent life)
He wont to hold companionship so free,
So pure, so fraught with knowledge and delight
As to be likened in his Followers' minds
To that which our first Parents, ere the fall . . .
Held with all Kinds in Eden's blisful bowers.

Lines Written in Early Spring

I heard a thousand blended notes,
    while in a grove I sate reclined,
In that sweet mood when pleasant thoughts
Bring sad thoughts to the mind.

To her fair works did Nature link
The human soul that through me ran;
And much it grieved my heart to think
What man has made of man.

Through primrose tufts, in that green bower,
The periwinkle trailed its wreaths;
And 'tis my faith that every flower
Enjoys the air it breathes.

The birds around me hopped and played,
Their thoughts I cannot measure: —
But the least motion which they made,
It seemed a thrill of pleasure.

The budding twigs spread out their fan,
To catch the breezy air;
And I must think, do all I can,
That there was pleasure there.

If this belief from heaven be sent,
If such be Nature's holy plan,
Have I not reason to lament
What man has made of man?

Samuel Taylor Coleridge

[1772–1834]

From *The Rime of the Ancient Mariner*

(Part VII)

The Hermit
of the wood.

This Hermit good lives in that wood
which slopes down to the sea.
How loudly his sweet voice he rears!
He loves to talk with marineres
That come from a far countree.

He kneels at morn, and noon, and eve —
He hath a cushion plump:
It is the moss that wholly hides
That rotted old oak-stump.

The skiff-boat neared: I heard them talk,
'Why, this is strange, I trow!
Where are those lights so many and fair,
That signal made but now?'

Approacheth
the ship with
wonder.

'Strange, by my faith!' the Hermit said —
'And they answered not our cheer!
The planks looked warped! and see those sails,
How thin they are and sere
I never saw aught like to them,
Unless perchance it were.

Brown skeletons of leaves that lag
My forest-brook along;
When the ivy-tod is heavy with snow,
And the owlet whoops to the wolf below,
That eats the she-wolf's young.'

'Dear Lord! it hath a fiendish look' —
(The Pilot made reply)
'I am a-feared — 'Push on, push on!'
Said the Hermit cheerily.

The boat came closer to the ship,
But I nor spake nor stirred;
The boat came closer beneath the ship,
And straight a sound was heard.

The ship
suddenly
sinketh.
Under the water it rumbled on
Still louder and more dread:
It reached the ship, it split the bay;
The ship went down like lead.

The ancient
Mariner is
saved in the
Pilot's boat.
Stunned by that loud and dreadful sound,
Which sky and ocean smote,
Like one that hath been seven days drowned
My body lay afloat;
But swift as dreams, myself I found
Within the Pilot's boat.

Upon the whirl, where sank the ship,
The boat spun round and round;
And all was still, save that the hill
Was telling of the sound.

I moved my lips — the Pilot shrieked
And fell down in a fit;
The holy Hermit raised his eyes,
And prayed where he did sit.

I took the oars: the Pilot's boy,
Who now doth crazy go,
Laughed loud and long, and all the while
His eyes went to and fro.
'Ha! ha!' quoth he, 'full plain I see,
The Devil knows how to row.'

And now, in all my own countree,
I stood on the firm land!

The Hermit stepped forth from the boat,
And scarcely he could stand.

'O shrive me, shrive me, holy man!'
The Hermit crossed his brow.
'Say quick,' quoth he, 'I bid thee say —
What manner of man art thou?'
Shrive him;

Forthwith this frame of mine was wrenched
With a woeful agony,
Which forced me to begin my tale;
And then it left me free.

Since then, at an uncertain hour,
That agony returns:
And till my ghastly tale is told,
This heart within me burns.

I pass, like night, from land to land;
I have strange power of speech;
That moment that his face I see,
I know the man that must hear me:
To him my tale I teach.

What loud uproar bursts from that door!
The wedding-guests are there:
But in the garden-bower the bride
And bride-maids singing are:
And hark the little vesper bell,
Which biddeth me to prayer!

O Wedding-Guest! this soul hath been
Alone on a wide wide sea:
So lonely 'twas, that God himself
Scarce seemèd there to be.

O sweeter than the marriage-feast,
'Tis sweeter far to me,
To walk together to the kirk
With a goodly company! —

To walk together to the kirk,
And all together pray,
While each to his great Father bends,
Old men, and babes, and loving friends,
And youths and maidens gay!

And to teach,
by his own
example, love
and reverence
to all things
that God made
and loveth.

Farewell, farewell! but this I tell
To thee, thou Wedding-Guest!
He prayeth well, who loveth well
Both man and bird and beast.

He prayeth best, who loveth best
All things both great and small;
For the dear God who loveth us,
He made and loveth all.

The Mariner, whose eye is bright,
Whose beard with age is hoar,
Is gone: and now the Wedding-Guest
Turned from the bridegroom's door.

He went like one that hath been stunned
And is of sense forlorn:
A sadder and a wiser man,
He rose the morrow morn.

To Nature

It may indeed be phantasy when I
Essay to draw from all created things
Deep, heartfelt, inward joy that closely clings:
And trace in leaves and flowers that round me lie
Lessons of love and earnest piety.
So let it be; and if the wide world rings
In mock of this belief, to me it brings
Nor fear, nor grief, nor vain perplexity.

So will I build my altar in the fields,
And the blue sky my fretted dome shall be,
And the sweet fragrance that the wild flower yields
Shall be the incense I will yield to Thee,
Thee only God! and Thou shalt not despise
Even me, the priest of this poor sacrifice.

Robert Southey

[1774–1843]

On the Death of a Spaniel

Ah, poor companion! when thou followedst last
Thy master's parting footsteps to the gate
Which closed for ever on him, thou did'st lose
Thy best friend, and none was left to plead
For the old age of brute fidelity.
But fare thee well. Mine is no narrow creed,
And He who gave thee being did not frame
The mystery of Life to be the sport
Of merciless man. There is another world
For all that live and move — a better one!
Where the proud bipeds, who would fain confine
Infinite goodness to the little bounds
Of their own charity, may envy thee.

George Gordon, Lord Byron

[1788–1824]

Inscription on the Monument of a Newfoundland Dog

When some proud son of man returns to earth,
Unknown to glory, but upheld by birth,
The sculptor's art exhausts the pomp of woe,

And storied urns record who rest below:
When all is done, upon the tomb is seen,
Not what he was, but what he should have been:
But the poor dog, in life the firmest friend,
The first to welcome, foremost to defend,
Whose honest heart is still his master's own,
Who labours, fights, lives, breathes for him alone,
Unhonour'd falls, unnoticed all his worth,
Denied in heaven the soul he held on earth:
While man, vain insect! hopes to be forgiven,
And claims himself a sole exclusive heaven.
Oh man! thou feeble tenant of an hour,
Debased by slavery, or corrupt by power,
Who knows thee well must quit thee with disgust,
Degraded mass of animated dust!
Thy love is lust, thy friendship all a cheat,
Thy smiles hypocrisy, thy words deceit!
By nature vile, ennobled but by name,
Each kindred brute might bid thee blush for shame.
Ye! who perchance behold this simple urn,
Pass on — it honours none you wish to mourn:
To mark a friend's remains these stones arise;
I never knew but one, — and here he lies.

—— Alphonse Marie Louis de Lamartine ——

[1790–1869]

From *Jocelyn's Episode*

My dog! the difference between thee and me
Knows only our Creator; — only He
Can number the degrees in being's scale
Between thy instinctive lamp, ne'er known to fail,
And that less steady light of brighter ray,
The soul which animates thy master's clay;

And He alone can tell by what fond tie,
My look thy life — my death, thy sign to die.
Howe'er this be, the human heart bereaved,
In thy affection owns a boon received;
Nor e'er, fond creature, prostrate on the ground,
Could my foot spurn thee or my accents wound.
No! never, never, my poor humble friend,
Could I by act or word thy love offend!
Too much in thee I reverence that Power
Which formed us both for our appointed hour;
That hand which links, by a fraternal tie,
The meanest of His creatures with the high.
Oh, my poor Fido! when thy speaking face,
Upturned to mine, of words supplies the place;
When, seated by my bed, the slightest moan
That breaks my troubled sleep, disturbs thine own;
When noting in my heavy eye the care
That clouds my brow, thou seek's its meaning there
And then, as if to chase that care away,
My pendant hand dost gently gnaw in play;
When, as in some clear mirror, I descry
My joys and griefs reflected in thine eye:
When tokens such as these thy reason speak
(Reason, which with thy love compared, is weak),
I cannot, will not, deem thee a deceiving,
Illusive mockery of human feeling,
A body organised, by fond caress
Warmed into seeming tenderness
A mere automaton, on which our love
Plays, as on puppets, when their wires we move.
No! when that feeling quits thy glazing eye,
'Twill live in some bliss world beyond the sky.

*   *   *   *   *   *

No! God will never quench His spark divine
Whether within some glorious orb it shine,
Or lighten up the spaniel's tender gaze,
Who leads his poor blind master through the maze
Of this dark world; and, when that task is o'er,
Sleeps on his humble grave, to wake no more.

—— Percy Bysshe Shelley ——

[1792–1822]

The Woodman and the Nightingale

A woodman whose rough heart was out of tune
(I think such hearts yet never came to good)
Hated to hear, under the stars or moon,

One nightingale in an interfluous wood
Satiate the hungry dark with melody;
And as a vale is watered by a flood,

Or as the moonlight fills the open sky
Struggling with darkness — as a tuberose
Peoples some Indian dell with scents which lie

Like clouds above the flower from which they rose,
The singing of that happy nightingale
In this sweet forest, from the golden close

Of evening till the star of dawn may fail,
Was interfused upon the silentness;
The folded roses and the violets pale

Heard her within their slumbers, the abyss
Of heaven with all its planets; the dull ear
Of the night-cradled earth; the loneliness

Of the circumfluous waters, — every sphere
And every flower and beam and cloud and wave,
And every wind of the mute atmosphere,

And every beast stretched in its rugged cave,

And every bird lulled on its mossy bough,
And every silver moth fresh from the grave

Which is its cradle — ever from below
Aspiring like one who loves too fair, too far,
To be consumed within the purest glow

Of one serene and unapproached star,
As if it were a lamp of earthly light,
Unconscious, as some human lovers are,

Itself how low, how high beyond all height
The heaven where it would perish! — and every form
That worshipped in the temple of the night

Was awed into delight, and by the charm
Girt as with an interminable zone,
Whilst that sweet bird, whose music was a storm

Of sound, shook forth the dull oblivion
Out of their dreams; harmony became love
In every soul but one.

* * * *

And so this man returned with axe and saw
At evening close from killing the tall treen,
The soul of whom by Nature's gentle law
Was each a wood-nymph, and kept ever green
The pavement and the roof of the wild copse,
Chequering the sunlight of the blue serene

With jagged leaves, — and from the forest tops
Singing the winds to sleep — or weeping oft
Fast showers of aereal water-drops

Into their mother's bosom, sweet and soft,
Nature's pure tears which have no bitterness; —
Around the cradles of the birds aloft

They spread themselves into the loveliness
Of fan-like leaves, and over pallid flowers
Hang like moist clouds: — or, where high branches kiss,

73

Make a green space among the silent bowers,
Like a vast fane in a metropolis,
Surrounded by the columns and the towers

All overwrought with branch-like traceries
In which there is religion — and the mute
Persuasion of unkindled melodies.

Odours and gleams and murmurs, which the lute
Of the blind pilot-spirit of the blast
Stirs as it sails, now grave and now acute,

Wakening the leaves and waves, ere it has passed
To such brief unison as on the brain
One tone, which never can recur, has cast,
One accent never to return again.

* * * * * * * * * *

The world is full of Woodmen who expel
Love's gentle Dryads from the haunts of life,
And vex the nightingales in every dell.

—— John Clare ——

[1793–1864]

The Robin

Now the snow hides the ground, little birds leave the
wood, and fly to the cottage to beg for their food;
While the robin, domestic, more tame than the rest,
With its wings drooping down, and rough feathers undrest,
Comes close to our windows, as much as to say,
'I would venture in, if I could find a way:
I'm starv'd, and I want to get out of the cold;
Oh! make me a passage, and think me not bold.'

Ah, poor little creature! thy visits reveal
Complaints such as these to the heart that can feel;
Nor shall such complainings be urged in vain;
I'll make thee a hole, if I take out a pane.
Come in, and a welcome reception thou'lt find;
I keep no grimalkin to murder inclin'd.
But oh, little robin! be careful to shun
That house, where the peasant makes use of a gun;
For if thou but taste of the seed he has strew'd,
Thy life as a ransom must pay for the food:
His aim is unerring, his heart is as hard,
And thy race, though so harmless, he'll never regard.
Distinction with him, boy, is nothing at all;
Both the wren, and the robin, with sparrows must fall.
For his soul (though he outwardly looks like a man)
Is in nature a wolf of the Apennine clan;
Like them his whole study is bent on his prey:
Then be careful, and shun what is meant to betray.
Come, come to my cottage, and thou shalt be free
To perch on my finger and sit on my knee:
Thou shalt eat of the crumbles of bread to thy fill,
And have leisure to clean both thy feathers and bill.
Then come, little robin! and never believe
Such warm invitiations are meant to deceive:
In duty I'm bound to show mercy on thee,
Since God don't deny it to sinners like me.

To the Snipe

L over of swamps
   and quagmire overgrown
With hassock-tufts of sedge, where fear encamps
   Around thy home alone,

   The trembling grass
   Quakes from the human foot,
Nor bears the weight of man to let him pass
   Where thou, alone and mute,

   Sittest at rest
   In safety, near the clump

Of huge flag-forest that thy haunts invest
Or some old sallow stump,

Thriving on seams
That tiny islands swell,
Just hilling from the mud and rancid streams,
Suiting thy nature well;

For here thy bill,
Suited by wisdom good,
Of rude unseemly length, doth delve and drill
The jellied mass for food;

And here, mayhap,
When summer suns have drest
The moor's rude, desolate and spongy lap,
May hide thy mystic nest —

Mystic indeed;
For isles that oceans make
Are scarcely more secure for birds to build
Than this flag-hidden lake.

Boys thread the woods
To their remotest shades;
But in these marshy flats, these stagnant floods,
Security pervades.

From year to year
Places untrodden lie,
Where man nor boy nor stock hath ventured near,
Naught gazed on but the sky

And fowl that dread
The very breath of man,
Hiding in spots that never knew his tread,
A wild and timid clan,

Widgeon and teal
And wild duck — restless lot,
That from man's dreaded sight, the water fowl,
Hide and are frightened not.

'Tis power divine
That heartens them to brave
The roughest tempest and at ease recline
On marshes or the wave.

Yet instinct knows
Not safety's bounds: — to shun
The firmer ground where skulking fowler goes
With searching dogs and gun,

By tepid springs
Scarcely one stride across
(Though bramble from its edge a shelter flings
Thy safety is at loss)

— And never choose
The little sinky foss,
Streaking the moors whence spa-red water spews
From pudges fringed with moss;

Freebooters there,
Intent to kill or slay,
Startle with cracking guns the trepid air,
And dogs thy haunts betray.

From danger's reach
Here thou art safe to roam,
Far as these washy flag-sown marshes stretch
A still and quiet home.

In these thy haunts
I've gleaned habitual love;
From the vague world where pride and folly taunts
I muse and look above.

Thy solitudes
The unbounded heaven esteems,
And here my heart warms into higher moods
And dignifying dreams.

I see the sky
Smile on the meanest spot,

Giving to all that creep or walk or fly
A calm and cordial lot.

Thine teaches me
Right feelings to employ —
That in the dreariest places peace will be
A dweller and a joy.

From *The Parish: A Satire*

Young Headlong Racket's to the last akin,
who only deals more openly in sin,
And apes forged love with less mysterious guile,
A high-flown dandy in its lowest style;
By fashion hated, with the vulgar gay,
He deems it wit to tempt their steps astray.
No maid can pass him but his leering eye
Attempts to prove her forward or too shy.
He brags o'er wine of loves his wits have won,
And loves betrayed — and deems it precious fun.
Horses and dogs and women o'er his wine
Is all his talk, and he believes it fine;
And fools may join him, but to common sense
His head pleads empty and has no pretence.
He courts his maids and shuns the better sort,
And hunts and courses as a change of sport,
And hates all poachers, game-destroying brutes,
Altho' with both the name as aptly suits,
With this one difference — darkness brings their prey,
And he more brazen murders his by day.
And thus he lives a hated sort of life,
Loves wedded wantons while he scorns a wife,
Prepares by turns to hunt and whore and shoot,
Less than a man and little more than brute.

Nature's Hymn to the Deity

All nature owns with one accord
the great and universal Lord:
The sun proclaims him through the day,

The moon when daylight drops away,
The very darkness smiles to wear
The stars that show us God is there,
On moonlight seas soft gleams the sky,
And, 'God is with us,' waves reply.

Winds breathe from God's abode, 'We come,'
Storms louder own God is their home,
And thunder yet with louder call,
Sounds, 'God is mightiest over all';
Till earth, right loath the proof to miss,
Echoes triumphantly, 'He is,'
And air and ocean makes reply,
'God reigns on earth, in air and sky.'

All nature owns with one accord
The great and universal Lord:
Insect and bird and tree and flower —
The witnesses of every hour —
Are pregnant with his prophecy
And, 'God is with us,' all reply.
The first link in the mighty plan
Is still — and all upbraideth man.

Badger

When midnight comes a host of dogs and men
go out and track the badger to his den,
And put a sack within the hole, and lie
Till the old grunting badger passes by.
He comes and hears — they let the strongest loose.
The old fox hears the noise and drops the goose.
The poacher shoots and hurries from the cry,
And the old hare half wounded buzzes by.
They get a forked stick to bear him down
And clap the dogs and take him to the town,
And bait him all the day with many dogs,
And laugh and shout and fright the scampering hogs.
He runs along and bites at all he meets:
They shout and holla down the noisy streets.

He turns about to face the loud uproar
And drives the rebels to their very door.
The frequent stone is hurled where'er they go;
When badgers fight, then every one's a foe.
The dogs are clapt and urged to join the fray;
The badger turns and drives them all away.
Though scarcely half as big, demure and small,
He fights with dogs for hours and beats them all.
The heavy mastiff, savage in the fray,
Lies down and licks his feet and turns away.
The bulldog knows his match and waxes cold,
The badger grins and never leaves his hold. He drives the
    crowd and follows at their heels
And bites them through — the drunkard swears and reels.

The frightened women take the boys away,
The blackguard laughs and hurries on the fray.
He tries to reach the woods, an awkward race,
But sticks and cudgels quickly stop the chase.
He turns agen and drives the noisy crowd
And beats the many dogs in noises loud.
He drives away and beats them every one,
And then they loose them all and set them on.
He falls as dead and kicked by boys and men,
Then starts and grins and drives the crowd agen;
Till kicked and torn and beaten out he lies
And leaves his hold and cackles, groans, and dies.

The Mole-Catcher

Tatterred and ragg'd, with greatcoat tied in strings,
   and collared up to keep his chin from cold,
The old mole-catcher on his journey sings,
Followed by shaggy dog infirm and old,
Who potters on and keeps his steady pace;
He is so lame he scarce can get abroad
But hopples on and growls at anything;
Yet silly sheep will scarcely leave the road.
With stick and spud he tried the new-made hills
And bears his cheating traps from place to place;
Full many are the miners that he kills.

His trotting dog oft looks him in the face;
And when his toils are done he tries to play
And finds a quicker pace and barks him on his way.

—— John Keats ——

[1795–1821]

From *Isabella*

With her two brothers this fair lady dwelt,
    enriched from ancestral merchandize,
And for them many a weary hand did swelt
    In torched mines and noisy factories,
And many once proud-quiver'd loins did melt
    In blood from stinging whip — with hollow eyes
Many all day in dazzling river stood,
To take the rich-ored driftings of the flood.

For them the Ceylon diver held his breath,
    And went all naked to the hungry shark;
For them his ears gush'd blood; for them in death
    The seal on the cold ice with piteous bark
Lay full of darts; for them alone did seethe
    A thousand men in troubles wide and dark:
Half-ignorant, they turn'd an easy wheel,
That set sharp racks at work, to pinch and peel.

Thomas Hood

[1799–1845]

A Butcher

Whoe'er has gone thro' London street
has seen a butcher gazing at his meat,
And how he keeps
Gloating upon a sheep's
Or bullock's personals, as if his own;
How he admires his halves
And quarters, and his calves.
As if in truth upon his own legs grown —
His fat, *his* suet,
His kidneys peeping elegantly thro' it,
His thick flank, and *his* thin,
His shank, *his* shin,
Skin of his skin, and bone too of his bone!

With what an air
He stands aloof across the thoroughfare
Gazing, and will not let a body by,
Tho' *buy, buy, buy*! be constantly his cry.
Meanwhile with arms akimbo, and a pair
Of Rhodian legs, he revels in a stare
At his Joint Stock — for one may call it so,
Howbeit with a *Co.*
The dotage of self-love was never fonder
Than he of his brute bodies all a-row;
Narcissus in the wave did never ponder,
With love so strong,
On his *portrait charmant*,
As our vain Butcher on his carcass yonder.

82

Look at his sleek round skull!
How bright his cheek, how rubicund his nose is!
   His visage seems to be
   Ripe for beef-tea;
Of brutal juices the whole man is full.
In fact, fulfilling the metempsychosis,
   The Butcher is already half a Bull.

On Richard Martin

(Richard Martin, 1754–1834, was MP for
Galway and introduced the first successful
   legislation to protect animals in 1822.)

How many sing of wars,
   Of Greek and Trojan jars —
The butcheries of men!
The Muse hath a 'Perpetual ruby pen,'
Dabbling with heroes and the blood they spill.
But no-one signs the man
That, like a pelican,
Nourishes Pity with his tender Bill,
Thou Wilberforce of hacks!
Of whites as well as blacks,
Piebald and dapple-grey,
Chestnut and bay —
No poet's eulogy thy name adorns,
But oxen from the fens,
Sheep in their pens,
Praise thee, and red cows with winding horns!

—— Henry Wadsworth Longfellow ——

[1807–1882]

The Emperor's Bird's Nest

Once the Emperor Charles of Spain,
  with his swarthy, grave commanders,
I forget in what campaign,
Long besieged, in mud and rain,
  Some old frontier town of Flanders.

Up and down the dreary camp,
  In great boots of Spanish leather,
Striding with a measured tramp,
These Hidalgos, dull and damp,
  Cursed the Frenchmen, cursed the weather.

Thus as to and fro they went,
  Over upland and through hollow,
Giving their impatience vent,
Perched upon the Emperor's tent,
  In her nest, they spied a swallow.

Yes, it was a swallow's nest,
  Built of clay and hair of horses,
Man, or tail, or dragoon's crest,
Found on hedgerows east and west,
  After skirmish of the forces.

Then an old Hidalgo said,
  As he twirled his grey mustachio,
'Sure this swallow overhead
Thinks the Emperor's tent a shed,
  And the Emperor but a Macho!'

Hearing his imperial name
  Coupled with those words of malice,
Half in anger, half in shame,
Forth the great campaigner came
  Slowly from his canvas palace.

'Let no hand the bird molest,'
  Said he solemnly, 'nor hurt her!'
Adding then, by way of jest,
'Golondrina is my guest,
  'Tis the wife of some deserter!'

Swift as bowstring speeds a shaft,
  Through the camp was spread the rumour,
And the soldiers, as they quaffed
Flemish beer at dinner, laughed
  At the Emperor's pleasant humour.

So unharmed and unafraid
  Sat the swallow still and brooded,
Till the constant cannonade
Through the walls a breach had made
  And the siege was thus concluded.

Then the army, elsewhere bent,
  Struck its tents as if disbanding,
Only not the Emperor's tent,
For he ordered, ere he went,
  Very curtly, 'Leave it standing!'

So it stood there all alone,
  Loosely flapping, torn and tattered,
Till the brood was fledged and flown,
Singing o'er those walls of stone
  Which the cannon-shot had shattered.

The Poet's Tale:
The Birds of Killingworth

It was the season, when through all the land
  The merle and mavis build, and building sing

Those lovely lyrics, written by His hand,
  Whom Saxon Caedmon calls the Blitheheart King;
When on the boughs the purple buds expand,
  The banners of the vanguard of the Spring,
  And rivulets, rejoicing, rush and leap,
And wave their fluttering signals from the steep.

The robin and the bluebird, piping loud,
  Filled all the blossoming orchards with their glee;
The sparrows chirped as if they still were proud
  Their race in Holy Writ should mentioned be;
And hungry crows assembled in a crowd,
  Clamoured their piteous prayer incessantly,
Knowing who hears the ravens cry, and said:
'Give us, O Lord, this day our daily bread!'

Across the Sound the birds of passage sailed,
  Speaking some unknown language strange and sweet
Of tropic isle remote, and passing hailed
  The village with the cheers of all their fleet;
Or quarrelling together, laughed and railed
  Like foreign sailors, landed in the street
Of seaport town, and with outlandish noise
Or oaths and gibberish frightening girls and boys.

Thus came the jocund Spring in Killingworth,
  In fabulous days, some hundred years ago;
And thrifty farmers, as they tilled the earth,
  Heard with alarm the cawing of the crow,
That mingled with the universal mirth,
  Cassandra-like, prognosticating woe;
They shook their heads, and doomed with dreadful words
To swift destruction the whole race of birds.

And a town-meeting was convened straightway
  To set a price upon the guilty heads
Of these marauders, who, in lieu of pay,
  Levied blackmail upon the garden beds
And cornfields, and beheld without dismay
  The awful scarecrow, with his fluttering shreds;
The skeleton that waited at their feast,
Whereby their sinful pleasure was increased.

Then from his house, a temple painted white,
   With fluted columns, and a roof of red,
The Squire came forth, august and splendid sight!
   Slowly descending, with majestic tread,
Three flights of steps, nor looking left nor right,
   Down the long street he walked, as one who said,
'A town that boasts inhabitants like me
Can have no lack of good society!'

The Parson, too, appeared, a man austere,
   The instinct of whose nature was to kill;
The wrath of God he preached from year to year,
   And read, with fervour, Edwards on the Will;
His favourite pastime was to slay the deer
   In summer on some Adirondac hill;
E'en now, while walking down the rural lane,
He lopped the wayside lilies with his cane.

From the Academy, whose belfry crowned
   The hill of Science with its vane of brass,
Came the Preceptor, gazing idly round,
   Now at the clouds, and now at the green grass,
And all absorbed in reveries profound
   Of fair Almira in the upper class,
Who was, as in a sonnet he had said,
As pure as water, and as good as bread.

And next the Deacon issued from his door,
   In his voluminous neckcloth white as snow;
A suit of sable bombazine he wore;
   His form was ponderous, and his step was slow;
There never was so wise a man before;
   He seemed the incarnate 'Well, I told you so!'
And to perpetuate his great renown
There was a street named after him in town.

These came together in the new town-hall,
   With sundry farmers from the region round.
The Squire presided, dignified and tall,
   His air impressive and his reasoning sound:
Ill fared it with the birds, both great and small;
   Hardly a friend in all that crowd they found,

But enemies enough, who every one
Charged them with all the crimes beneath the sun.

When they had ended, from his place apart,
    Rose the Preceptor, to redress the wrong,
And, trembling like a steed before the start,
    Looked round bewildered on the expectant throng:
Then thought of fair Almira, and took heart
    To speak out what was in him, clear and strong,
Alike regardless of their smile or frown,
And quite determined not to be laughed down.

'Plato, anticipating the Reviewers,
    From his Republic banished without pity
The Poets; in this little town of yours,
    You put to death, by means of a Committee,
The ballad-singers and the Troubadours,
    The street-musicians of the heavenly city, —
The birds, — who make sweet music for us all
In our dark hours, as David did for Saul.

'The thrush that carols at the dawn of day
    From the green steeples of the piny wood;
The oriole in the elm; the noisy jay,
    Jargoning like a foreigner at his food;
The bluebird balanced on some topmost spray,
    Flooding with melody the neighbourhood;
Linnet and meadow-lark, and all the throng
That dwells in nests, and have the gift of song.

'You slay them all!' and wherefore? for the gain
    Of a scant handful more or less of wheat,
Or rye, or barley, or some other grain,
    Scratched up at random by industrious feet,
Searching for worm or weevil after rain!
    Or a few cherries, that are not so sweet
As are the songs these uninvited guests
Sing at their feast with comfortable breasts.

'Do you ne'er think what wondrous beings these?
    Do you ne'er think who made them, and who taught
The dialect they speak, where melodies

Alone are the interpreters of thought?
Whose household words are songs in many keys,
   Sweeter than instrument of man e'er caught!
Whose habitations in the tree-tops even
Are half-way houses on the road to heaven!

'Think, every morning when the sun peeps through
   The dim, leaf-latticed windows of the grove,
How jubilant the happy birds renew
   Their old, melodious madrigals of love!
And when you think of this, remember too
   'Tis always morning somewhere, and above
The awakening continents, from shore to shore,
Somewhere the birds are singing evermore.

'Think of your woods and orchards without birds!
   Of empty nests that cling to boughs and beams
As in an idiot's brain remembered words
   Hang empty 'mid the cobwebs of his dreams!
Will bleat of flocks or bellowing of herds
   Make up for the lost music, when your teams
Drag home the stingy harvest, and no more
The feathered gleaners follow to your door?

'What! would you rather see the incessant stir
   Of insects in the windows of the hay,
And hear the locust and the grasshopper
   Their melancholy hurdy-gurdies play?
Is this more pleasant to you than the whir
   Of meadow-lark, and her sweet roundelay,
Or twitter of little field-fares, as you take
Your nooning in the shade of bush and brake?

'You call them thieves and pillagers; but know,
   They are the winged wardens of your farms,
Who from the cornfields drive the insidious foe,
   And from your harvests keep a hundred harms;
Even the blackest of them all, the crow,
   Renders good service as your man-at-arms,
Crushing the beetle in his coat of mail,
And crying havoc on the slug and snail.

'How can I teach your children gentleness,
    And mercy to the weak, and reverence,
For Life, which, in its weakness or excess,
    Is still a gleam of God's omnipotence,
Or Death, which, seeming darkness, is no less
    The self-same light, although averted hence,
When by your laws, your actions, and your speech,
You contradict the very things I teach?'

With this he closed; and through the audience went
    A murmur, like the rustle of dead leaves;
The farmers laughed and nodded, and some bent
    Their yellow heads together like their sheaves;
Men have no faith in fine-spun sentiment
    Who put their trust in bullocks and in beeves.
The birds were doomed; and, as the record shows,
A bounty offered for the heads of crows.

There was another audience out of reach,
    Who had no voice nor vote in making laws,
But in the papers read his little speech,
    And crowned his modest temples with applause;
They made him conscious, each one more than each,
    He still was victor, vanquished in their cause.
Sweetest of all the applause he won from thee
Of fair Almira at the Academy!

And so the dreadful massacre began;
    O'er fields and orchards, and o'er woodland crests,
The ceaseless fusillade of terror ran.
    Dead fell the birds, with bloodstains on their breasts,
Or wounded crept away from sight of man,
    While the young died of famine in their nests;
A slaughter to be told in groans, not words,
The very St. Bartholomew of Birds!

The Summer came, and all the birds were dead;
    The days were like hot coals; the very ground
Was burned to ashes; in the orchards fed
    Myriads of caterpillars, and around
The cultivated fields and gardenbeds.
    Hosts of devouring insects crawled, and found

No foe to check their march, till they had made
The land a desert without leaf or shade.

Devoured by worms, like Herod, was the town,
   Because, like Herod, it had ruthlessly
Slaughtered the Innocents. From the trees spun down
   The cankerworms upon the passers-by,
Upon each woman's bonnet, shawl, and gown,
   Who shook them off with just a little cry;
They were the terror of each favourite walk,
The endless theme of all the village talk.

The farmers grew impatient, but a few
   Confessed their error, and would not complain,
For after all, the best thing one can do
   When it is raining, is to let it rain.
Then they repealed the law, although they knew
   It would not call the dead to life again;
As schoolboys, finding their mistake too late
Draw a wet sponge across the accusing slate.

That year in Killingworth the Autumn came
   Without the light of his majestic look,
The wonder of the falling tongues of flame,
   The illumined pages of his Doomsday book.
A few lost leaves blushed crimson with their shame,
   And drowned themselves despairing in the brook,
While the wild wind went moaning everywhere,
Lamenting the dead children of the air!

But the next Spring, a stranger sight was seen,
   A sight that never yet by bard was sung,
As great a wonder as it would have been
   If some dumb animal had found a tongue!
A wagon, overarched with evergreen,
   Upon whose boughs were wicker cages hung,
All full of singing birds, came down the street,
Filling the air with music wild and sweet.

From all the country round these birds were brought,
   By order of the town, with anxious quest,
And, loosened from their wicker prisons, sought

In woods and fields the places they loved best,
Singing loud canticles, which many thought
    Were satires to the authorities addressed,
While others, listening in green lanes, averred
Such lovely music never had been heard!

But blither still and louder carolled they
    Upon the morrow, for they seemed to know
It was the fair Almira's wedding-day,
    And everywhere, around, above, below,
When the Preceptor bore his bride away,
    Their songs burst forth in joyous overflow,
And a new heaven bent over a new earth
Amid the sunny farms of Killingworth.

The Sermon of St. Francis

Up soared the lark into the air,
    a shaft of song, a winged prayer,
As if a soul, released from pain,
Were flying back to heaven again.

St Francis heard; it was to him
An emblem of the Seraphim;
The upward motion of the fire,
The light, the heat, the heart's desire.

Around Assisi's convent gate
The birds, God's poor who cannot wait,
From moor and mere and darksome wood
Came flocking for their dole of food.

'O brother birds,' St. Francis said,
'Ye come to me and ask for bread,
But not with bread alone to-day
Shall ye be fed and sent away.

'Ye shall be fed, ye happy birds,
With manna of celestial words;
Not mine, though mine they seem to be,
Not mine, though they be spoken through me.

92

'O, doubly are ye bound to praise
The great Creator in your lays;
He giveth you your plumes of down,
Your crimson hoods, your cloaks of brown.

'He giveth you your wings to fly
And breathe a purer air on high,
And careth for you everywhere,
Who for yourselves so little care!'

With flutter of swift wings and songs
Together rose the feathered throngs,
And singing scattered far apart;
Deep peace was in St. Francis' heart.

He knew not if the brotherhood
His homily had understood;
He only knew that to one ear
The meaning of his words was clear.

—— John Greenleaf Whittier ——

[1807–1892]

The Robin

My old Welsh neighbor over the way
    crept slowly out in the sun of spring,
Pushed from her ears the locks of gray,
    And listened to hear the robin sing.

Her grandson, playing at marbles, stopped,
    And, cruel in sport as boys will be,
Tossed a stone at the bird, who hopped
    From bough to bough in the apple-tree.

'Nay!' said the grandmother; 'have you not heard,
    My poor, bad boy! of the fiery pit,
And how, drop by drop, this merciful bird
    Carries the water that quenches it?

'He brings cool dew in his little bill,
    And lets it fall on the souls of sin:
You can see the mark on his red breast still
    Of fires that scorch as he drops it in.

'My poor Bron rhuddyn! my breast-burned bird,
    Singing so sweetly from limb to limb,
Very dear to the heart of Our Lord
    Is he who pities the lost little Him!'

'Amen!' I said to the beautiful myth;
    'Sing, bird of God, in my heart as well:
Each good thought is a drop wherewith
    To cool and lessen the fires of hell.

'Prayers of love like rain-drops fall,
    Tears of pity are cooling dew,
And dear to the heart of Our Lord are all
    Who suffer like Him in the good they do!'

A Dream of Summer

Bland as the morning breath of June
    the southwest breezes play;
And, through its haze, the winter noon
    Seems warm as summer's day.
The snow-plumed Angel of the North
    Has dropped his icy spear;
Again the mossy earth looks forth,
    Again the streams gush clear.

The fox his hillside cell forsakes,
    The muskrat leaves his nook,
The bluebiird in the meadow brakes
    Is singing with the brook.
'Bear up, O Mother Nature!' cry

94

Bird, breeze, and streamlet free;
'Our winter voices prophesy
   of summer days to thee!'

So, in those winters of the soul,
   By bitter blasts and drear
O'erswept from Memory's frozen pole,
   Will sunny days appear.
Reviving Hope and Faith, they show
   The soul its living powers,
And how beneath the winter's snow
   Lie germs of summer flowers!

The Night is mother of the Day,
   The Winter of the Spring,
And ever upon old Decay
   The greenest mosses cling.
Behind the cloud the starlight lurks,
   Through showers the sunbeams fall;
For God, who loveth all His works,
   Has left His hope with all!

How the Robin Came:
An Algonquin Legend

Happy young friends, sit by me,
   under May's blown apple-tree,
While these home-birds in and out
Through the blossoms flit about.
Hear a story, strange and old,
By the wild red Indians told,
How the robin came to be:
Once a great chief left his son, —
Well-beloved, his only one, —
When the boy was well-nigh grown,
In the trial-lodge alone.
Left for tortures long and slow
Youths like him must undergo,
Who their pride of manhood test,
Lacking water, food, and rest.

Seven days the fast he kept,
Seven nights he never slept.
Then the young boy, wrung with pain,
Weak from nature's overstrain,
Faltering, moaned a low complaint;
'Spare me, father, for I faint!'
But the chieftain, haughty-eyed,
Hid his pity in his pride.
'You shall be a hunter good,
Knowing never lack of food:
You shall be a warrior great,
Wise as fox and strong as bear;
Many scalps your belt shall wear,
If with patient heart you wait
Bravely till your task is done.
Better you should starving die
Than that boy and squaw should cry
Shame upon your father's son!'

When next morn the sun's first rays
Glistened on the hemlock sprays,
Straight that lodge the old chief sought,
And boiled samp and moose meat brought.
'Rise and eat, my son!' he said.
Lo, he found the poor body dead!
As with grief his grave they made,
And his bow beside him laid,
Pipe, and knife, and wampum-braid,
On the lodge-top overhead,
Preening smooth its breast of red
And the brown coat that it wore,
Sat a bird, unknown before.
And as if with human tongue,
'Mourn me not,' it said, or sung;
'I, a bird, am still your son,
Happier than if hunter fleet,
Or a brave, before your feet
Laying scalps in battle won.
Friend of man, my song shall cheer
Lodge and corn-land; hovering near,
To each wigwam I shall bring
Tidings of the coming spring;

Every child my voice shall know
In the moon of melting snow,
When the maple's red bud swells,
And the wind-flower lifts its bells.
As their fond companion
Men shall henceforth own your son,
And my song shall testify
That of human kin am I.'

Thus the Indian legend saith
How, at first, the robin came
With a sweeter life from death,
Bird for boy, and still the same.
If my young friends doubt that this
Is the robin's genesis,
Not in vain is still the myth
If a truth be found therewith;
Unto gentleness belong
Gifts unknown to pride and wrong;
Happier far than hate is praise, —
He who sings than he who slays.

The Worship of Nature

The harp at Nature's advent strung
    Has never ceased to play;
The song the stars of morning sung
    Has never died away.

And prayer is made, and praise is given,
    By all things near and far;
The ocean looketh up to heaven,
    And mirrors every star.
Its waves are kneeling on the strand,
    As kneels the human knee,
Their white locks bowing to the sand,
    The priesthood of the sea!

They pour their glittering treasures forth,
    Their gifts of pearl they bring,
And all the listening hills of earth
    Take up the song they sing.

The green earth sends her incense up
    From many a mountain shrine;
From folded leaf and dewy cup
    She pours her sacred wine.

The mists above the morning rills
    Rise white as wings of prayer;
The altar-curtains of the hills
    Are sunset's purple air.

The winds with hymns of praise are loud,
    Or low with sobs of pain, —
The thunder-organ of the cloud,
    The dropping tears of rain.

With drooping head and branches crossed
    The twilight forest grieves,
Or speaks with tongues of Pentecost
    From all its sunlit leaves.

The blue sky is the temple's arch,
    Its transept earth and air,
The music of its starry march
    The chorus of a prayer.

So Nature keeps the reverent frame
    With which her years began,
And all her signs and voices shame
    The prayerless heart of man.

Charles Tennyson Turner

[1801–1879]

To a starved Hare in
the Garden in Winter

Soft-footed stroller from the herbless wood,
  Stealing so mutely through my garden ground,
I will not balk thine eager quest for food,
Nor take thy life, nor startle thee with sound.
I spared the wanton squirrel, though I saw
His autumn raid upon my nuts and cones;
I spared his frisky brush and bushy jaw;
And shall I wound the poor dishearten'd ones?
Come freely: in my heart thy charter lies;
Feed boldly — what thou gain'st I cannot lose.
When robin shuffles on the snow-white sill,
We serve his winsome hunger; who would choose
To daunt his ruddy breast and wistful eyes?
But, hare or robin, it is hunger still.

On Shooting a Swallow in Early Youth

I hoard a little spring of secret tears,
  For thee, poor bird; thy death-blow was my crime:
From the far past it has flow'd on for years;
It never dries; it brims at swallow-time.
No kindly voice within me took thy part,
Till I stood o'er thy last faint flutterings;
Since then, methinks, I have a gentler heart,
And gaze with pity all on wounded wings.
Full oft the vision of thy fallen head,
Twittering in highway dust, appeals to me;

Thy helpless form, as when I struck thee dead,
Drops out from every swallow-flight I see.
I would not have thine airy spirit laid,
I seem to love the little ghost I made.

The Cattle Train
Penmaenmawr

All light or transient gloom — no hint of storm —
white wreaths of foam, born in blue waters, broke
Among the mountain shadows; all bespoke
A summer's day on Mona and the Orme.
My open window overlook'd the rails,
When, suddenly, a cattle-train went by,
Rapt, in a moment, from my pitying eye,
As from their lowing mates in Irish vales;
Close-pack'd and mute they stood, as close as bees,
Bewilder'd with their fright and narrow room;
'Twas sad to see that meek-eyed hecatomb,
So fiercely hurried past our summer seas,
Our happy bathers, and our fresh sea-breeze,
And hills of blooming heather, to their doom.

Cynotaphium

When some dear human friend to death doth bow,
Fair blooming flowers are strewn upon the bier,
And haply, in the silent house, we hear
The last wild kiss ring on the marble brow,
And lips that never miss'd reply till now;
And thou, poor dog, wert in thy measure dear —
And so I owe thee honour, and the tear
Of friendship, and would all thy worth allow.
In a false world, thy heart was brave and sound;
So, when my spade carved out thy latest lair,
A spot to rest thee on, I sought and found —
It was a tuft of primrose, fresh and fair,
And, as it was thy last hour above ground,
I laid thy sightless head full gently there.
'I cannot think thine all is buried here,'

I said, and sigh'd — the wind awoke and blew
The morning-beam along the gossamer,
That floated o'er thy grave all wet with dew;
A hint of better things, however slight,
Will feed a loving hope; it soothed my woe
To watch that little shaft of heavenly light
Pass o'er thee, moving softly to and fro:
Within our Father's heart the secret lies
Of this dim world; why should *we only* live
And what was I that I should close mine eyes
On all those rich presumptions, that reprieve
The meanest life from dust and ashes? Lo!
How much on such dark ground a gleaming thread can do!

Silent Praise

O Thou, Who givest to the woodland wren
    A throat, like to a little light-set door,
That opens to his early joy — to men
The spirit of true worship, which is more
Than all this sylvan rapture: what a world
Is Thine, O Lord! — skies, earth, men, beasts, and birds!
The poet and the painter have unfurl'd
Their love and wonder in descriptive words,
Or sprightly hues — each, after his own sort,
Emptying his heart of its delicious hoards;
But all self-conscious blazonry comes short
Of that still sense no active mood affords,
Ere yet the brush is dipt, or utter'd phrase
Hath breathed abroad those folds of silent praise!

Alfred, Lord Tennyson

[1809–1892]

From *In Memoriam*

(Part Liv*)*

Oh yet we trust that somehow good
    will be the final goal of ill,
  To pangs of nature, sins of will,
Defects of doubt, and taints of blood;

That nothing walks with aimless feet;
    That no one life shall be destroy'd,
    Or cast as rubbish to the void,
When God hath made the pile complete;

That not a worm is cloven in vain;
    That not a moth with vain desire
    Is shrivell'd in a fruitless fire,
Or but subserves another's gain.

Behold, we know not anything;
    I can but trust that good shall fall
    At last — far off — at last, to all,
And every winter change to spring.

So runs my dream: but what am I?
    An infant crying in the night:
    An infant crying for the light:
And with no language but a cry.

Robert Browning

[1812–1889]

Tray

Sing me a hero! Quench my thirst
　　of soul, ye bards!
　　Quoth Bard the first:
'Sir Olaf, the good knight, did don
His helm and eke his habergeon . . .'
Sir Olaf and his bard ——!

'That sin-scathed brow' (quoth Bard the second)
'that eye wide open as though Fate beckoned
My hero to some steep, beneath
Which precipice smiled tempting death . . .'
You too without your host have reckoned!

'A beggar-child' (let's hear this third!)
'Sat on a quay's edge: like a bird
Sang to herself at careless play,
And fell into the stream. 'Dismay!
Help, you the standers-by!' None stirred.

'Bystanders reason, think of wives
And children ere they risk their lives.
Over the balustrade has bounced
A mere instinctive dog, and pounced
Plumb on the prize. 'How well he dives!

'Up he comes with the child, see, tight
In mouth, alive took, clutched from quite
A depth of ten feet — twelve, I bet!
Good dog! What, off again? There's yet
Another child to save? All right!

'How strange we saw no other fall!
It's instinct in the animal.
Good dog! But he's a long while under:
If he got drowned I should not wonder —
Strong current, that against the wall!

'Here he comes, holds in mouth this time
— What may the thing be? Well, that's prime!
Now, did you ever? Reason reigns
In man alone, since all Tray's pains
Have fished — the child's doll from the slime!

And so, amid the laughter gay,
Trotted my hero off, — old Tray, —
Till somebody, prerogatived
With reason, reasoned: 'Why he dived,
His brain would show us, I should say.

'John, go and catch — or, if needs be,
Purchase that animal for me!
By vivisection, at expense
Of half-an-hour and eighteenpence,
How brain secretes dog's soul, we'll see!'

—— Walt Whitman ——

[1819–1892]

Miracles

Why, who makes much of a miracle?
As to me I know of nothing else but miracles,
Whether I walk the streets of Manhattan,
Or dart my sight over the roofs of houses toward the sky,
Or wade with naked feet along the beach just in the edge
     of the water,

Or stand under trees in the woods,
Or talk by day with any one I love, or sleep in the bed at
    night with any one I love,
Or sit at table at dinner with the rest,
Or look at strangers opposite me riding in the car,
Or watch honey-bees busy around the hive of a summer fore-
    noon
Or animals feeding in the fields,
Or birds, or the wonderfulness of insects in the air,
Or the wonderfulness of the sundown, or of stars shining so
    quiet and bright,
Or the exquisite delicate thin curve of the new moon in
    spring;
These with the rest, one and all, are to me miracles,
The whole referring, yet each distinct and in its place.
To me every hour of the light and dark is a miracle,
Every cubic inch of space is a miracle,
Every square yard of the surface of the earth is spread with
    the same,
Every foot of the interior swarms with the same.

To me the sea is a continual miracle,
The fishes that swim — the rocks — the motion of the
    waves — the ships with men in them,
What stranger miracles are there?

From *Song of Myself*

I think I could turn and live with animals, they are so
    placid and self-contain'd,
I stand and look at them long and long.

They do not sweat and whine about their condition,
They do not lie awake in the dark and weep for their sins,
They do not make me sick discussing their duty to God,
Not one is dissatisfied, not one is demented with the mania
    of owning things,

Not one kneels to another, nor to his kind that lived
    thousands of years ago,
Not one is respectable or unhappy over the whole earth.

— Matthew Arnold —

[1822–1888]

On the Death of a Favourite Canary

Poor Matthias! Wouldst thou have
    more than pity? claim'st a stave?
— Friends more near us than a bird
We dismiss'd without a word.
Rover, with the good brown head,
Great Atossa, they are dead;
Dead, and neither prose nor rhyme
Tells the praises of their prime.
Thou dist know them old and gray,
Know them in their sad decay.
Thou hast seen Atossa sage
Sit for hours beside thy cage;
Thou wouldst chirp, thou foolish bird,
Flutter, chirp – she never stirr'd;
What were now these toys to her?
Down she sank amid her fur;
Eyed thee with a soul resign'd —
And thou deemedst cats were kind!
— Cruel, but composed and bland,
Dumb, inscrutable and grand,
So Tiberius might have sat,
Had Tiberius been a cat.

    Birds, companions more unknown,
Live beside us, but alone;

Finding not, do all they can,
Passage from their souls to man.
Kindness we bestow, and praise,
Laud their plumage, greet their lays;
Still, beneath their feather'd breast,
Stirs a history unexpress'd.
Wishes there, and feelings strong,
Incommunicably throng;
What they want, we cannot guess,
Fail to track their deep distress —
Dull look on when death is nigh,
Note no change, and let them die.

Was it as the Grecian sings,
Birds were born the first of things,
Before the sun, before the wind,
Before the gods, before mankind,
Airy, ante-mundane throng —
Witness their unworldly song!
Proof they give, too, primal powers,
Of a prescience more than ours —
Teach us, while they come and go,
When to sail, and when to sow.
Cuckoo calling from the hill,
Swallow skimming by the mill;
Swallows trooping in the sedge,
Starlings swirling from the hedge,
Mark the seasons, map our year,
As they show and disappear.
But, with all this travail sage
Brought from that anterior age,
Goes an unreserved decree
Whereby strangers are they and we,
Making want of theirs, and plan,
Indiscernible by man.

Ralph Waldo Emerson

[1830–1882]

To the Humble-Bee

Burly, dozing humble-bee,
  where thou art is clime for me.
Let them sail for Porto Rique,
Far-off heats through seas to seek;
I will follow thee alone,
Thou animated torrid-zone/
Zigzag steerer, desert cheerer,
Let me chase thy waving lines;
Keep me nearer, me thy hearer,
Singing over shrubs and vines.

Insect lover of the sun,
Joy of thy dominion!
Sailor of the atmosphere;
Swimmer through the waves of air;
Voyager of light and noon;
Epicurean of June;
Wait, I prithee, till I come
Within earshot of thy hum,—
All without is martyrdom.

When the south wind, in May days,
With a net of shining haze
Silvers the horizon wall,
And, with softness touching all,
Tints the human countenance
With a colour of romance,
And, infusing subtle heats,
Turns the sod to violets,

Thou, in sunny solitudes,
Rover of the underwoods,
The green silence dost displace
With thy mellow, breezy bass.

Hot midsummer's petted crone!
Sweet to me thy drowsy tone
Tells of countless sunny hours,
Long days, and solid banks of flowers;
Of gulfs of sweetness without bound
In Indian wildernesses found;
Of Syrian peace, immortal leisure,
Firmest cheer, and bird-like pleasure.

Aught unsavoury or unclean
Hath my insect never seen;
But violets and bilberry bells,
Maple-sap, and daffodels,
Grass with green flag half-mast high,
Succory to match the sky,
Columbine with horn of honey,
Scented fern, and agrimony,
Clover, catchfly, adder's-tongue,
And brier-roses dwelt among;
All beside was unknown waste,
All was picture as he passed.

Wiser far than human seer,
Yellow-breeched philosopher!
Seeing only what is fair,
Sipping only what is sweet,
Thou dost mock as fate and care,
Leave the chaff, and take the wheat.
When the fierce northwestern blast
Cools sea and land so far and fast,
Thou already slumberest deep;
Woe and want thou canst outsleep;
Want and woe, which torture us,
Thy sleep makes ridiculous.

109

The Birds

Darling of children and of bard,
 perfect kinds by vice unmarred,
All of worth and beauty set
Gems in Nature's cabinet;
These the fables she esteems
Reality most like to dreams.
Welcome back, you little nations,
Far-travelled in the south plantations;
Bring your music and rhythmic flight,
Your colors for our eyes' delight:

Freely nestle in our roof,
Weave your chamber weatherproof
And your enchanting manners bring
And your autumnal gathering.
Exchange in conclave general
Greetings kind to each and all,
Conscious each of duty done
And unstainèd as the sun.

From *Woodnotes*

Ever fresh the broad creation,
 a divine improvisation,
From the heart of God proceeds,
A single will, a million deeds.
Once slept the world an egg of stone,
And pulse, and sound, and light was none;
And God said, 'Throb!' and there was motion
And the vast mass became vast ocean.
Onward and on, the eternal Pan,
Who layeth the world's incessant plan,
Halteth never in one shape,
But forever doth escape,
Like wave or flame, into new forms
Of gem, and air, of plants, and worms . . .

He is the essence that inquires.
He is the axis of the star;

He is the sparkle of the spar;
He is the heart of every creature;
He is the meaning of each feature;
And his mind is the sky.
Than all it holds more deep, more high.

—— Thomas Hardy ——

[1840–1928]

Last Words to a Dumb Friend

Pet was never mourned as you,
  purrer of the spotless hue,
Plumy tail, and wistful gaze
While you humoured our queer ways,
Or outshrilled your morning call
Up the stairs and through the hall —
Foot suspended in its fall —
While, expectant, you would stand
Arched to meet the stroking hand;
Till your way you chose to wend
Yonder, to your tragic end.

Never another pet for me!
Let your place all vacant be;
Better blankness day by day
Than companion torn away.
Better bid his memory fade,
Better blot each mark he made,
Selfishly escape distress
By contrived forgetfulness,
Than preserve his prints to make
Every morn and eve an ache.

111

From the chair whereon he sat
Sweep his fur, nor wince thereat;
Rake his little pathways out
Mid the bushes roundabout;
Smooth away his talons' mark
From the claw-worn pine-tree bark,
Where he climbed as dusk embrowned,
Waiting us who loitered round.

Strange it is this speechless thing,
Subject to our mastering,
Subject for his life and food
To our gift, and time, and mood;
Timid pensioner of us Powers,
His existence ruled by ours,
Should — by crossing at a breath
Into safe and shielded death,
By the merely taking hence
Of his insignificance —
Loom as largened to the sense,
Shape as part, above man's will,
Of the Imperturbable.

As a prisoner, flight debarred,
Exercising in a yard,
Still retain I, troubled, shaken,
Mean estate, by him forsaken;
And this home, which scarcely took
Impress from his little look,
By his faring to the Dim
Grows all eloquent of him.

Housemate, I can think you still
Bounding to the window-sill,
Over which I vaguely see
Your small mound beneath the tree,
Showing in the autumn shade
That you moulder where you played.

The Puzzled Game-Birds

They are not those who used to feed us
   when we were young — they cannot be —
These shapes that now bereave and bleed us?
They are not those who used to feed us,
For did we then cry, they would heed us.
— If hearts can house such treachery
They are not those who used to feed us
When we were young — they cannot be!

A Sheep Fair

The day arrives of the autumn fair,
   and torrents fall,
Though sheep in throngs are gathered there,
   Ten thousand all,
Sodden, with hurdles round them reared:
And, lot by lot, the pens are cleared,
And the auctioneer wrings out his beard,
And wipes his book, bedrenched and smeared,
And rakes the rain from his face with the edge of his hand,
   As torrents fall.

The wool of the ewes is like a sponge
   With the daylong rain:
Jammed tight, to turn, or lie, or lunge,
   They strive in vain.
Their horns are soft as finger-nails,
Their shepherds reek against the rails,
The tied dogs soak with tucked-in tails,
The buyers' hat-brims fill like pails,
Which spill small cascades when they shift their stand
   In the daylong rain.

Postscript

Time has trailed lengthily since met
At Pummery Fair

Those panting thousands in their wet
  And woolly wear:
And every flock long since has bled,
And all the dripping buyers have sped,
  And the hoarse auctioneer is dead,
  Who 'Going — going!' so often said,
As he consigned to doom each meek, mewed band
  At Pummery Fair.

Bags of Meat

'Here's a fine bag of meat,'
  Says the master-auctioneer,
  As the timid, quivering steer,
  Starting a couple of feet
  At the prod of a drover's stick,
  And trotting lightly and quick,
  A ticket stuck on his rump,
Enters with a bewildered jump.

'Where he's lived lately, friends,
  I'd live till lifetime ends:
  They've a whole life everyday
  Down there in the Vale, have they!
  He'd be worth the money to kill
And give away Christmas for good-will.'

'Now here's a heifer — worth more
  Than bid, were she bone-poor;
  Yet she's round as a barrel of beer;'
'She's a plum,' said the second auctioneer.

'Now this young bull — for thirty pound?
  Worth that to manure your ground!'
  'Or to stand,' chimed the second one,
  'And have his picter done!'
The beast was rapped on the horns and snout
  To make him turn about.
'Well,' cried a buyer, 'another crown —
Since I've dragged here from Taunton Town!'

114

'That calf, she sucked three cows,
    Which is not matched for bouse
    In the nurseries of high life
By the first-born of a nobleman's wife!'
The stick falls, meaning, 'A true tale's told,'
On the buttock of the creature sold,
    And the buyer leans over and snips
His mark on one of the animal's hips.

    Each beast, when driven in,
Looks round at the ring of bidders there
With a much-amazed reproachful stare,
    As at unnatural kin,
For bringing him to a sinister scene
So strange, unhomelike, hungry, mean;
His fate the while suspended between
    A butcher, to kill out of hand,
    And a farmer, to keep on the land;
One can fancy a tear runs down his face
When the butcher wins, and he's driven from the place.

The Blinded Bird

So zestfully canst thou sing?
    and all this indignity,
With God's consent, on thee!
Blinded ere yet a-wing
By the red-hot needle thou,
I stand and wonder how
So zestfully thou canst sing!

Resenting not such wrong,
Thy grievous pain forgot,
Eternal dark thy lot,
Groping thy whole life long,
After that stab of fire;
Enjailed in pitiless wire;
Resenting not such wrong!

Who hath charity? This bird.
Who suffereth long and is kind,
Is not provoked, though blind

115

And alive ensepulchred?
Who hopeth, endureth all things?
Who thinketh no evil, but sings?
Who is divine? This bird.

Compassion:
An Ode
In Celebration of the Centenary of the Royal Society
for the Prevention of Cruelty to Animals

I

Backward among the dusky years
   A lonesome lamp is seen arise,
  Lit by a few fain pioneers
    Before incredulous eyes. —
  We read the legend that it lights:
'Wherefore beholds this land of historied rights
Mild creatures, despot-doomed, bewildered, plead
Their often hunger, thirst, pangs, prisonment,
   In deep dumb gaze more eloquent
    Than tongues of widest heed?'

II

What was faint-written, read in a breath
In that year — ten times ten away —
A larger louder conscience saith
  More sturdily to-day. —
But still those innocents are thralls
To throbless fears, near, far, that hear no calls
Of honour towards their too-dependent frail,
And from Columbia Cape to Ind we see
  How helplessness breeds tyranny
   In power above assail.

III

  Cries still are heard in secret nooks,
  Till hushed with gag or slit or thud;
  And hideous dens whereon none looks
   Are sprayed with needless blood.

116

But here, in battlings, patient, slow,
Much has been won — more, maybe, than we know —
And on we labour hopeful. 'Ailinon!'
A mighty voice calls: 'But may the good prevail!'
  And 'Blessed are the merciful!'
    Calls a yet mightier one.

The Lady in Furs

'I'm a lofty lovely woman,'
  Says the lady in the furs,
In the glance she throws around her
  On the poorer dames and sirs:
'This robe, that cost three figures,
  Yes, is mine,' her nod avers.

'True, my money did not buy it,
  But my husband's, from the trade;
And they, they only got it
  From things feeble and afraid
By murdering them in ambush
  With a cunning engine's aid.

'True, my hands, too, did not shape it
  To the pretty cut you see,
But the hands of midnight workers
  Who are strangers quite to me:
It was fitted, too, by dressers
  Ranged around me toilsomely.

'But I am a lovely lady,
  Though sneerers say I shine
By robbing Nature's children
  Of apparel not mine,
And that I am but a broom-stick,
  Like a scarecrow's wooden spine.'

The Mongrel

In Havenpool Harbour the ebb was strong,
And a man with a dog drew near and hung,

117

And taxpaying day was coming along,
   So the mongrel had to be drowned.
The man threw a stick from the paved wharf-side
Into the midst of the ebbing tide,
And the dog jumped after with ardent pride
   To bring the stick aground.

But no: the steady suck of the flood
To seaward needed, to be withstood,
More than the strength of mongrelhood
   To fight its treacherous trend.
So, swimming for life with desperate will,
The struggler with all his natant skill
Kept buoyant in front of his master, still
   There standing to wait the end.

The loving eyes of the dog inclined
To the man he held as a god enshrined,
With no suspicion in his mind
   That this had all been meant.
Till the effort not to drift from shore
Of his little legs grew slower and slower,
And, the tide still outing with brookless power,
   Outward the dog, too, went.

Just ere his sinking what does one see
Break on the face of that devotee?
A wakening to the treachery
   He had loved with love so blind?
The faith that had shone in that mongrel's eye
That his owner would save him by and by
Turned to much like a curse as he sank to die,
   And a loathing of mankind.

118

Gerard Manley Hopkins

[1844–1889]

God's Grandeur

The world is charged with the grandeur of God.
  It will flame out, like shining from shook foil;
  It gathers to a greatness, like the ooze of oil
Crushed. Why do men then now not reck his rod?
Generations have trod, have trod, have trod;
  And all is seared with trade; bleared, smeared with toil;
  And whereas man's smudge and shares man's smell: the soil
Is bare now, nor can foot feel, being shod.

And for all this, nature is never spent:
  There lives the dearest freshness deep down things;
And though the last lights off the black West went
  Oh, morning, at the brown brink eastward, springs —
Because the Holy Ghost over the bent
  World broods with warm breast and with ah! bright wings.

Pied Beauty

Glory be to God for dappled things —
    for skies of couple-colour as a brinded cow;
  For rose-moles all in stipple upon trout that swim;

Fresh-firecoal chestnut falls; finches' wings;
  Landscape plotted and pieced — fold, fallow, and plough;
  And all trades, their gear and tackle and trim.

All things counter, original, spare, strange
  Whatever is fickle, freckled (who knows how?)

119

With swift, slow; sweet, sour; adazzle, dim,
He fathers-forth whose beauty is past change:
Praise him.

The Caged Skylark

As a dare-gale skylark scanted in a dull cage
       man's mounting spirit in his bone-house, mean house,
dwells —
    That bird beyond the remembering his free fells;
This in drudgery, day-labouring-out life's age.

Though aloft on turf or perch or poor low stage,
    Both sing sometimes the sweetest, sweetest spells,
    Yet both droop deadly sometimes in their cells
Or wring their barriers in bursts of fear or rage.

Not that the sweet-fowl, song-fowl, needs no rest —
Why, hear him, hear him babble and drop down to his nest,
    But his own nest, wild nest, no prison.

Man's spirit will be flesh-bound when found at best,
But uncumbered: meadow-down is not distressed
    For a rainbow footing it nor he for his bones risen.

—— Ella Wheeler Wilcox ——

[1850–1919]

Kinship

I am the voice of the voiceless;
    Through me the dumb shall speak,
Till the deaf world's ear be made to hear
    The wrongs of the worldless weak.

From street, from cage and from kennel,
  From stable and zoo, the wail
Of my tortured kin proclaims the sin
  Of the mighty against the frail.

Oh, shame on the mothers of mortals,
  Who have not stooped to teach
Of the sorrow that lies in dear, dumb eyes,
  The sorrow that has no speech.

The same force formed the sparrow
  That fashioned man the king;
The God of the whole gave a spark of soul
  To furred and to feathered thing.

And I am my brother's keeper,
  And I will fight his fight,
And speak the word for beast and bird,
  Till the world shall set things right.

—— Henry Salt ——

[1851–1939]

The Pious Angler
(The Izaak Walton Window in Winchester Cathedral)

'The quaint old cruel coxcomb in his gullet
  Should have a hook, and a small trout to pull it.'
'Twas Byron's thought; but now, more highly prized,
Behold the Pious Angler canonized!
The Saint, who fixed his frog upon the hook
As if he loved him, and with tender look
The writhing worm would prayerfully impale!
So let the tinted window tell the tale,

121

Staining the great cathedral's marble floor
With pale red radiance, thin as fishes' gore.
There, amid holy martyrs, shall he stand,
With halo on his head, and rod in hand,
Musing on Nature's joys (but most, his dish);
God's fisherman, cold-blooded as God's fish.

'A Bird in the Hand'

'A bird in hand, worth two in bush,' you say.
Not if in Nature's scales their worth we weigh.
She loves the bush, abhors the aviary;
Rates high o'er captive eagle sparrow free;
Thinks not her tameless children to enthral;
Your 'bird in hand' is scarce a bird at all.

'Calf Love'

Calf-love's a soft romantic fire,
The young and amorous feel;
Not that indelicate desire,
Man's appetite for veal.

'Accounted For'
('The stag was finally accounted for')

'Accounted for'! How nice it sounds
compared with 'stuck' or 'shot'!
You'd think a stag pursued by hounds
Had enviable lot.
But those who hunted him? Would they,
The folk so gaily mounted,
Enjoy the sport and 'Hark away'
If they, too, were 'accounted'?

A Lover of Animals

Oh, yes! You love them well, I know!
    But whisper me — when most?
'In fields, at summer-time.' Not so:
    At supper-time — in roast.

'He' and 'It'

(Strange fact, that the English language makes all animals of the neuter
gender.' Schopenhauer)

'He' was a man, a worthless wight,
    Who drank, and knew no shame,
Till, reckless, on some frenzied night,
    He set his house aflame.

'It' was a dog that instant ran,
    By faithful love made brave;
How base soe'er might be the man,
    A master's life to save.

'A gallant dog!' the neighbours cried,
    And praised such canine wit;
Then, wondering, spread the story wide
    How 'he' was saved by 'it'!

To Metchnikoff, The Civilizer

('His inoculation of anthropoid apes with syphilis was successful.' *Life of
Elie Metchnikoff*)

Hail, Metchnikoff, great master-mind,
    Whose thought the Future shapes!
Thou first did'st civilize mankind
    By syphilizing apes.

John Galsworthy

[1867–1933]

A Little Serval Cat

I knew a little Serval cat —
  never get out!
Would pad all day from this to that —
  Never get out!
From bar to bar she'd turn and turn
  And in her eyes a fire would burn —
  (From her, Zoology we learn!)
    Never get out!

And if by hap a ray of sun
Came shining in her cage, she'd run
And sit upon her haunches, where
In the open she would stare,
And with the free that sunlight share —
  Never get out!

That catling's jungle heart forlorn
Will die as wild as it was born.
If I could cage the human race
Awhile, like her, in prisoned space,
And teach them what it is to face
  Never get out!

G. K. Chesterton

[1874–1936]

The Donkey

When fishes flew and forests walked,
   and figs grew upon thorn,
Some moment when the moon was blood
   Then surely I was born;

With monstrous head and sickening cry
   And ears like errant wings,
The devil's walking parody
   On all four-footed things.

The tattered outlaw of the earth
   Of ancient crooked will;
Starve, scourge, deride me: I am dumb,
   I keep my secret still.

Fools! For I also had my hour;
   One far fierce hour and sweet;
There was a shout about my ears,
   And palms before my feet.

Edward Thomas

[1878–1917]

The Gallows

There was a weasel lived in the sun
      with all his family,
Till a keeper shot him with his gun
And hung him up on a tree,
Where he swings in the wind and rain,
In the sun and in the snow,
Without pleasure, without pain
On the dead oak tree bough.

There was a crow who was no sleeper,
But a thief and a murderer
Till a very late hour; and this keeper
Made him one of the things that were,
To hang and flap in rain and wind,
In the sun and in the snow.
There are no more sins to be sinned
On the dead oak tree bough.

There was a magpie, too,
Had a long tongue and a long tail
He could both talk and do —
But what did that avail?
He, too, flaps in the wind and rain
Alongside weasel and crow,
Without pleasure, without pain,
On the dead oak tree bough.

And many other beasts
And birds, skin, bone and feather,

Have been taken from their feasts,
And hung up there together,
To swing and have endless leisure
In the sun and in the snow,
Without pain, without pleasure,
On the dead oak tree bough.

—— D. H. Lawrence ——

[1885–1930]

Snake

A snake came to my water-trough
On a hot, hot day, and I in pyjamas for the heat,
To drink there.

In the deep, strange-scented shade of the great dark
    carob-tree,
I came down the steps with my pitcher
And must wait, must stand and wait, for there he was at the
    trough before me.

He reached down from a fissure in the earth-wall in the
    gloom
And trailed his yellow-brown slackness soft-bellied down,
    over the edge of the stone trough
And rested his throat upon the stone bottom,
And where the water had dripped from the tap, in a small
    clearness,
He sipped with his straight mouth,
Softly drank through his straight gums, into his slack, long
    body,
Silently.

Someone was before me at my water trough,

And I, like a second comer, waiting.
He lifted his head from his drinking, as cattle do,
And looked at me vaguely, as drinking cattle do,
And flickered his two-forked tongue from his lips, and mused
    a moment,
And stooped and drank a little more,
Being earth-brown, earth-golden from the burning bowels of
    the earth
On the day of Sicilian July, with Etna smoking.

The voice of my education said to me
He must be killed,
For in Sicily the black, black snakes are innocent, the gold
    are venomous.

The voices in me said, If you were a man
You would take a stick and break him now, and finish him
    off.

But must I confess how I liked him,
How glad I was he had come as a guest in quiet, to drink
    at my water-trough
And depart peaceful, pacified, and thankless,
Into the burning bowels of this earth.

Was it cowardice, that I dared not kill him?
Was it perversity, that I longed to talk to him?
Was it humility, to feel so honoured?
I felt so honoured.
And yet those voices:
If you were not afraid, you would kill him!

And truly I was afraid, I was most afraid,
But even so, honoured still more
That he should seek my hospitality
From out the dark door of the secret earth.

He drank enough
And lifted his head, dreamily, as one who has drunken
And flickered his tongue like a forked night on the air,
    so black,
Seeming to lick his lips,

And looked around like a god, unseeing, into the air,
And slowly turned his head,
And slowly, very slowly, as if thrice adream,
Proceeded to draw his slow length curving round
And climb again the broken bank of my wall-face.

And as he put his head into that dreadful hole,
And as he slowly drew up, snake-easing his shoulders,
    and entered farther,
A sort of horror, a sort of protest against his withdrawing
    into that horrid black hole,
Deliberately going into the blackness, and slowly drawing
    himself after,
Overcame me now his back was turned.

I looked round, I put down my pitcher,
I picked up a clumsy log
And threw it at the water-trough with a clatter.
I think it did not hit him,
But suddenly the part of him that was left behind convulsed
    in undignified haste,
Writhed like lightning, and was gone
Into the black hole, the earth-lipped fissure in the wall-front,
At which, in the intense still noon, I stared with fascination.

And immediately I regretted it.
I thought how paltry, how vulgar, what a mean act!
I despised myself and the voices of my accursed human
    education.
And I thought of the albatross,
And I wished he would come back, my snake.

For he seemed to me again like a king,
Like a king in exile, uncrowned in the underworld,
Now due to be crowned again.

And so, I missed my chance with one of the lords
Of life.
And I have something to expiate;
A pettiness.

Mountain Lion

Climbing through the January snow, into the Lobo canyon
  Dark grow the spruce-trees, blue is the balsam, water
  sounds still unfrozen, and the trail is still evident
Men!
Two men!
Men! The only animal in the world to fear!

They hesitate.
We hesitate.
They have a gun.
We have no gun.

Then we all advance, to meet.

Two Mexicans, strangers, emerging out of the dark
  and snow and inwardness of the Lobo valley.
What are you doing here on this vanishing trail?

What is he carrying?
Something yellow.
A deer?

Qúe tiene, amigo?
Léon —

He smiles, foolishly, as if he were caught doing wrong.
And we smile, foolishly, as if we didn't know.
He is quite gentle and dark-faced.

It is a mountain lion,
A long, long slim cat, yellow like a lioness.
Dead.
He trapped her this morning, he says, smiling foolishly.

Lift up her face,
Her round, bright face, bright as frost.
Her round, fine-fashioned head, with two dead ears;
And stripes in the brilliant frost of her face, sharp,
    fine dark rays,

Dark, keen, fine eyes in the brilliant frost of her face.
Beautiful dead eyes.

Hermoso es!

They go out towards the open;
We go on into the gloom of Lobo.
And above the trees I found her lair,
A hole in the blood-orange brilliant rocks that stick up,
    a little cave.

And bones, and twigs, and a perilous ascent.

So, she will never leap up that way again, with the yellow
    flash of a mountain lion's long shoot!
And her bright striped frost-face will never watch any more,
    out of the shadow of the cave in the blood-orange rock,
Above the trees of the Lobo dark valley-mouth!

Instead, I look out,
And out to the dim of the desert, like a dream, never real;
To the snow of the Sangre de Cristo mountains, the ice of
    the mountains of Picoris,
And near across at the opposite steep of snow, green trees
    motionless standing in snow, like a Christmas toy.

And I think in this empty world there was room for me and
    a mountain lion.
And I think in the world beyond, how easily we might spare
    a million or two of humans
And never miss them.
Yet what gap in the world, the missing white frost-face of
    that slim yellow mountain lion!

Lizard

A lizard ran out on a rock and looked up, listening
  no doubt to the sounding of the spheres.
And what a dandy fellow! the right toss of a chin for you
and swirl of a tail!

If men were as much men as lizards are lizards
they'd be worth looking at.

—— Joseph Plunkett ——

[1887–1916]

I See His Blood upon the Rose

I see His blood upon the rose
  And in the stars the glory of His eyes,
His body gleams amid eternal snows,
His tears fall from the skies.

I see His face in every flower;
The thunder and the singing of the birds
Are but His voice—and carven by His power
Rocks are His written words.

All pathways by His feet are worn,
His strong heart stirs the ever-beating sea,
His crown of thorns is twined with every thorn,
His cross is every tree.

—— Edith Sitwell ——

[1887–1964]

Still Falls the Rain

(The Raids, 1940. Night and Dawn)

Still falls the Rain —
  Dark as the world of man, black as our loss —

Blind as the nineteen hundred and forty nails
Upon the Cross.

Still falls the Rain
With a sound like the pulse of the heart that is changed to
        the hammer-beat
In the Potters' Field, and the sound of the impious feet
On the Tomb:
    Still falls the Rain
In the Field of Blood where the small hopes breed and the
        human brain
Nurtures its greed, that worm with the brow of Cain.

Still falls the Rain
At the feet of the Starved Man hung upon the Cross.
Christ that each day, each night, nails there, have mercy
        upon us —
On Dives and on Lazarus:
Under the Rain the sore and the gold are as one.

Still falls the Rain —
Still falls the Blood from the Starved Man's wounded side
He bears in his Heart all wounds, — those of the light that
        died,
The last faint spark
In the self-murdered heart, the wounds of the sad
        uncomprehending dark,
The wounds of the baited bear, —
The blind and weeping bear whom the keepers beat
On his helpless flesh . . . the tears of the hunted hare.

Still falls the Rain —
Then — O I leape up to my God: who pulles me doune —
See, see where Christ's blood streames in the firmament:
It flows from the Brow we nailed upon the tree
Deep to the dying, to the thirsting heart
That holds the fires of the world, — dark-smirched with pain
At Caesar's laurel crown.

Then sounds the voice of One who like the heart of man
Was once a child who among beasts has lain —

'Still do I love, still shed my innocent light, my Blood,
    for thee.'

—— R. S. Thomas ——

[1931 –   ]

The White Tiger

It was beautiful as God
    must be beautiful; glacial
eyes that had looked on
violence and come to terms

with it; a body too huge
and majestic for the cage in which
it had been put; up
and down in the shadow

of its own bulk it went,
lifting, as it turned,
the crumpled flower of its face
to look into my own

fast without seeing me. It
was the colour of the moonlight
on snow and as quiet
as moonlight, but breathing

as you can imagine that
God breathes within the confines
of our definition of him, agonising
over immensities that will not return.

Alan Brownjohn

[1931–   ]

We are Going to See the Rabbit

We are going to see the rabbit,
we are going to see the rabbit.
Which rabbit, people say?
Which rabbit, ask the children?
Which rabbit?
The only rabbit,
The only rabbit in England,
Sitting behind a barbed-wire fence
Under the floodlights, neon lights,
Sodium lights,
Nibbling grass
On the only patch of grass
In England, in England
(Except the grass by the hoardings
Which doesn't count.)

And we must be there on time.

First we shall go by escalator,
Then we shall go by underground,
And then we shall go by motorway
And then by helicopterway
And the last ten yards we shall have to go
On foot.

And now we are going
All the way to see the rabbit,
We are nearly there,
We are longing to see it,

And so is the crowd
Which is here in thousands
With mounted policemen
And big loudspeakers
And bands and banners,
And everyone has come a long way.
But soon we shall see it
Sitting and nibbling
The blades of grass
On the only patch of grass
In — but something has gone wrong!
Why is everyone so angry,
Why is everyone jostling
And slanging and complaining?

The rabbit has gone,
Yes, the rabbit has gone.
He has actually burrowed down into the earth
And made himself a warren, under the earth,
Despite all these people,
And what shall we do?
What *can* we do?

It is all a pity, you must be disappointed,
Go home and do something else for today,
Go home again, go home for today.
For you cannot hear the rabbit under the earth,
Remarking rather sadly to himself, by himself,
As he rests in his warren under the earth:
'It won't be long, they are bound to come,
They are bound to come and find me, even here.'

Adrian Mitchell

[1932–   ]

Back in the Playground Blues

Dreamed I was in a school playground, I was about four
    feet high
Yes dreamed I was back in the playground, and
standing about four feet high
The playground was three miles long and the
        playground was five miles wide
It was broken black tarmac with a high fence all around
Broken black dusty tarmac with a high fence running
        all around
And it had a special name to it, they called it The
        Killing Ground.

Got a mother and a father, they're a thousand miles away
The Rulers of the Killing Ground are coming out to play
Everyone thinking: who they going to play with today?

You get it for being Jewish
Get it for being black
Get it for being chicken
Get it for fighting back
You get it for being big and fat
Get it for being small
O those who get it get it and get it
For any damn thing at all

Sometimes they take a beetle, tear off its six legs one by one
Beetle on its black back rocking in the lunchtime sun
But a beetle can't beg for mercy, a beetle's not half the fun

Heard a deep voice talking, it had that iceberg sound;
'It prepares them for Life' — but I have never found
Any place in my life that's worse than The Killing Ground.

—— Armorel Kay Walling ——

[20th Century]

Go Tell all Creatures in the World

Go tell all creatures in the world
    The Good News that I bring;
That was the message Jesus gave,
And He is Lord and King.

Let's tell it by the deeds we do;
In ways they understand:
Deal gently with the beasts and birds
Who share our Saviour's Land.

Protect His forests, heal the air,
Care for His shining sea,
Arrest our cruelty and greed
And set its victims free.

So shall our lives proclaim the One
Who sent a little child
To lead all things safe home, in Him
Redeemed and reconciled,

To where — upon His holy hill —
None hurt and none destroy
And all Creation's present groans
Are turned to songs of joy.

Easter

The world's full of blossoms
And the city seems,
Like winter, scarce of account.
The sudden glory of a resurrected sun
Brings forth the bumblebee, that old recluse,
With tales of miracles the faintest heart could not refuse.
And there is triumph in the mood
Which rocks the cheerful solitude.

Vesper

I wish that I, when evening comes
And shadows cannot hide the scars
Of man's destruction left across the land,
And cars go roaring lullabies —
Above the rush I wish
That I could yet be moved
To sing a song forgiving — like the thrush.

—— Virginia McKenna ——

[20th Century]

Solitude

I am in my room, alone.
Time is nothing.
The silence and its stillness pleases me.

I can keep this solitude
Without question,
Until the need to end it pleases me.

In his small cage, alone,
Time is nothing.
His silence is within, inside his brain,
He keeps this inward silence
To protect him
From eyes that do not understand his pain.

I keep him in this cage
My primate brother,
I keep him on display for all to see,
I must be sure that he knows
Who is master,
That in my hand, alone, lies freedom's key.

—— Brother Antoninus ——

[20th Century]

A Canticle to the Waterbirds
Written for the Feast of St Francis of Assisi, 1950

Clack your beaks you cormorants and kittiwakes,
    North on those rockcroppings fingerjutted into the
        rough Pacific surge;
    You migratory terns and pipers who leave but the
    temporal claw-track written on sandbars there of your
    presence;
Grebes and pelicans; you comber-picking scoters and you
        shore-long gulls;
All you keepers of the coastline north of here to the
        Mendocino beaches;
All you beyond upon the cliff-face thwarting the surf at
        Hecate Head,
Hovering the under-surge where the cold Columbia grapples
        at the bar;

140

North yet to the Sound, whose islands float like a sown flurry
    of chips upon the sea:
Break wide your harsh and salt-encrusted beaks unmade for
    song
And say a praise up to the Lord.

And you freshwater egrets east in the flooded marshlands
    skirting the sea-level rivers, white one-legged watchers
    of shallows;
Broadheaded kingfishers minnow-hunting from willow stems
    on meandering valley sloughs;
You too, you herons, blue and supple-throated, stately,
    taking the air majestical in the sunflooded San Joaquin,
Grading down on your belted wings from the upper lights
    on sunset,
Mating over the willow clumps or where the flatwater rice-
    fields shimmer;
You killdeer, high night criers, far in the moon-suffusion sky;
Bitterns, sandwaders, all shorewalkers, all roostkeepers,
Populates of the 'dobe cliffs of the Sacramento:
Open your waterdartling beaks,
And make a praise up to the Lord.

For you hold the heart of His mighty fastness,
And shape the life of His indeterminate realms.
You are everywhere on the lonesome shores of His wide
    creation.
You keep seclusion where no man may go, giving Him praise;
Nor may a woman come to lift like your cleaving fight her
    clear contralto song
To honor the spindrift gifts of His soft abundance.
You sanctify His hermitage rocks where no holy priest may
    kneel to adore, nor holy nun assist;
And where his true communion-keepers are not enabled to
    enter.
And well may you say His praises, birds, for your ways
Are verved with the secret skills of His inclinations,
And your habits plaited and rare with the subdued
    elaboration of His intricate craft;
Your days intent with the direct astuteness needful for His
    outworking

141

And your nights alive with the dense repose of His infinite
  sleep.
You are His secretive charges and you serve His secretive
  ends,
In His clouded mist-conditioned stations, in His murk,
Obscure in your matted nestings, immured in His limitless
  ranges.
He makes you penetrate through dark interstitial joinings of
  His thicketed kingdoms,
And keep your concourse in the keeps of His shadowed
  world.

Your ways are wild but earnest, your manners grave,
Your customs carefully schooled to the note of His serious
  mien.
You hold the prime condition of His clean creating,
And the swift compliance with which you serve His minor
  means
Speaks of the constancy with which you hold Him.
For what is your high flight forever going home to your first
  beginnings,
But such a testament to your devotion?
You hold His outstretched world beneath your wings, and
  mount upon His storms,
And keep your sheer wind-lidded sight upon the vast
  perspectives of His mazy latitudes.

But mostly it is your way you bear existence wholly within
  the context of His utter will and are untroubled.
Day upon day you do not reckon, nor scrutinize tomorrow,
  nor multiply the nightfalls with a rash concern,
But rather assume each instant as warrant sufficient of His
  final seal.
Wholly in Providence you spring, and when you die you look
  on death in clarity unflinched,
Go down, a clutch of feather ragged upon the brush;
Or drop on water where you briefly lived, found food,
And now yourselves made food for His deep current-keeping
  fish, and then are gone:
Is left but the pinion feather spinning a bit on the uproil
Where lately the dorsal cut clear air.

You leave a silence. And this for you suffices, who are not
    of the ceremonials of man,
And hence are not made sad to now forgo them.
Yours is of another order of being, and wholly it compels.
But you may, birds, utterly seized in God's supremacy,
Austerely living under His austere eye —
Yet may you teach a man a necessary thing to know,
Which has to do if the strict conformity that creaturehood
    entails,
And constitutes the prime commitment all things share.
For God has given you the imponderable grace to *be* His
    verification,
Outside the mulled incertitude of our forensic choices;
That you, our lessers in the rich hegemony of Being,
May serve as testament to what a creature is,
And what creation owes.

Curlews, stilts and scissortails, beachcomber gulls;
Wave-hunters, short-keepers, rockhead-holders, all cape-top
    vigilantes,
Now give God praise.
Send up the strict articulation of your throats,
And say His name.

—— Anon ——

[20th Century]

What Became of Them?

He was a rat, and she was a rat,
    and down in one hole they did dwell,
And both were as black as a witch's cat,
    And they loved one another well.

He had a tail, and she had a tail,

143

Both long and curling and fine;
And each said, 'Yours is the finest tail
  In the world, excepting mine.'
He smelt the cheese, and she smelt the cheese,
  And they both pronounced it good;
And both remarked it would greatly add
  To the charms of their daily food.

So he ventured out, and she ventured out,
  And I saw them go with pain;
But what befell them I never can tell,
  For they never came back again.

Jon Wynne–Tyson

[20th Century]

The Shooting Party

Strange the heart of man
  to spread sorrow on a dying land,
almost as though the season's flux,
the blind blood of beast and bird,
and all this rust-red mantle
hid insufficient pain.

How aberrant the hedgerow ape —
killing for no need,
maiming without remorse,
yet tightly proud of his hyena ways!

There may be justice lying in the land;
deep in the quiet earth, nature's mute revolt
breeds some distant scheme.
We get back from the sad soil
the harvest of our sowing.

Down the Road two Humans have been Murdered

Shot in their bed,
intruder unknown.
We met the couple; they have children.

Over the way a cow lows miserably
(three days now, day and night);
her calf's birth was a week ago
and painfully audible.

Down the road the police move slowly,
dabbing paintwork, glass,
busy with tapes and pegs.
Important deaths merit ritual.

The media speculate.
The bank-bound farmer leaves in his Jag.
Down the road two humans have been murdered;
over the way a cow lows.

Dog

Painfully conscious
of the pitfalls of sentiment
(the reminders are plentiful enough);
of too much imagination;
of (heaven help us) anthropomorphism;
I nevertheless, small animal —
even eschewing the soft brown eyes bit
and all the routine mush —
suspect I am more human
for your non-human company
than for all the proximity
of my two-legged friends.

Patrick Huddie

[20th Century]

Haydn's 'Creation'

'And God created great whales, and every living
  creature that moveth. And God blessed them saying:
Be fruitful and multiply'
  Be fruitful and multiply,
Vibrate this sonorous bass, these richly weaving strings —
Springing from Alpine meadows Papa Haydn, singing God's
      Word to his élitist crowds;
Be fruitful and multiply, move on the sensuous strings,
Singing of beasts on heat, genetic mysteries and barren
      overpopulated lands.
'Let copulation thrive' joins in old Lear, till sex
Without fruits without love flaunts out from every
      page and screen.
Self-consciously within their clothes these modern bodies
Sit, wrapt for a while in Haydn's warm embrace. Outside,
      quick insects
Fertilising flowers, and seed still reach their goal

Traveller

Am a tadpole waiting in the wings,
    now fish shot from a gun,
        athlete clustering on the track
        racing whiplash home

Now a pulsing jellyfish,
        berry seething in the bowl
        where rise, unfold like seahorse
        curl into rabbit

146

Then a blind and hooded raider
tapping impatient fingers
waiting
to break out

W. H. Vanstone

[20th Century]

A Hymn to the Creator

Morning glory, starlit sky,
　　Leaves in springtime, swallows' flight,
Autumn gales, tremendous seas,
Sounds and scents of summer night;

Soaring music, tow'ring words,
Art's perfection, scholar's truth,
Joy supreme of human love,
Memory's treasure, grace of youth;

Open, Lord are these, Thy gifts,
Gifts of love to mind and sense;
Hidden is love's agony,
Love's endeavour, love's expense.

Love that gives gives ever more,
Gives with zeal, with eager hands,
Spares not, keeps not, all outpours,
Ventures all, its all expends.

Drained is love in making full;
Bound in setting others free;
Poor in making many rich;
Weak in giving power to be.

147

Therefore He Who Thee reveals
Hangs, O Father, on that Tree
Helpless; and the nails and thorns
Tell of what Thy love must be.

Thou art God; no monarch Thou
Thron'd in easy state to reign;
Thou art God, Whose arms of love
Aching, spent, the world sustain.

—— Saiom Bertsch ——

[20th Century]

Number Forty One

(To Ethel Thurston of the American Fund
for Alternatives to Animal Research, NYC)

Was it misnumbered?
   this perfume numbered five?
take one part of ambergris
from a sperm whale
add some drops of castor
ripped from a Canadian beaver
and 1 civet cat rotated
in a drum to frighten it
into secreting hormones
and 38 musk oxen castrated
for 1 ounce of musk
. . . should this perfume be called Perfume No. 41?

148

Christian Cockroaches

(to Danuto of CBN who asked why
God made cockroaches)

'No room at the inn'
they said when His cockroaches
born

and in the middle of their
lives the creatures loved
by the Son of Man have
like Him no place to lay
their heads

and at the end
'Father Father why hast
Thou forsaken us' they
crie as they died, nailed
by the shoes of those
who could not see God
in his living temples

and then they flew to
Him from the vases . .
the shells . . the bodies
they'd left

—— Roger Woodis ——

[20th Century]

The Smell of Money

('The World About Us: The Musk Connection'
29 June, 1986, BBC2)

'Animals!' yell the demented headlines,
'Animals!' when they invade the pitch.

Animals don't understand the market,
Nor do they dream of becoming rich.

Those who live best in their quest for profit
Weigh up the worth of an ivory tusk;
Elegant people with polished faces
Have a keen nose for the price of musk.

Silly to blame them for being greedy,
Or to deny them their right to poach;
Harry the deer in the Himalayas,
All that you need is the right approach.

Never go calling the vendors villains,
Brand not the buyers in old Japan;
Musk is so sexy and musk means money —
Musk is a must for the husky man.

Would you mind dropping your sloppy values?
Here is a deer that produces gold.
Only one question requires an answer:
Not 'Is it filthy?' but 'Can it be sold?'

——— **Brother Ramon, SSF** ———

(20th Century)

Lamb on the Anelog Mountain

Perched on the side of the Anelog mountain
On the tip of the Lleyn Peninsula
Facing the numinous Island of Bardsey
Called Ynys Enlli, Island of twenty thousand saints,
Stands a soft, white, silent, woolly lamb.

Winter wind howls around the tiny cottage,
Mist swirls past, enveloping Anelog in clouds,
The rain is lashed by the wind,
But the lamb stands, wind-swept, wet and alone,
Looking towards my lighted window.

He does not initiate movement
But under the poor shelter of the low stone wall
Stands unsteadily, patiently, attentively,
Against the cold, wet buffeting,
Attracted by the movement of the window lamp.

Agnus Dei, qui tollis peccata mundi,
Lamb of God, by your very persistence,
By your patience, your expectation,
Your attention and concrete presence
You draw me to gaze through the window.

Miserere nobis — have mercy upon us.
Lamb of God, why do you stand so patiently
When I am so restless and uncertain?
Why do you gaze upon me so searchingly?
Is it reproach or silent yearning that you stand so?

Dona nobis pacem. The elements swirl about you,
Shrieking wind, soaking rain, and ragged mists,
Yet you stand patiently, offering me your peace,
Your silence bearing eloquent witness,
Your stillness enveloping you and me in mystery.

Dear lamb, why am I so immensely moved?
Why does my pulse quicken so?
Why do tears spring to my eyes?
Solitary lamb, straying on Anelog mountain,
In your presence I stand before the Lamb of God.

Cosmic Prayer (i) Unity and Harmony

When the frail body lays aside
Recurring, restless, active strife,
And when the mind withdraws from all

The world's demands and fretful strife,
And when the spirit's quiet and still,
There lies our peace — Your perfect will.

For when the body and the mind
Are in the spirit's strong control,
Disintegrated vital powers
Move towards their harmonious whole;
For body, mind and spirit move
Within the universal Love.

Love is the energy of life,
The fabric of the cosmic power,
And when we give ourselves to love
In every meditation hour
Its repercussion circles round
Re-echoing love's deep, mystic sound.

The body lives and moves and grows
Within the pattern of the whole,
Rooted in earth and sea and sky
It breathes within the cosmic soul;
God's Spirit moves within the earth
Bringing His life and love to birth.

The breath of God breathes through the world
Manifestation of His life;
We breath in rhythmic, glad response
In breathing peace, expelling strife,
Till spirit, mind and body free
Joy in such cosmic harmony.

(ii) The Bondage of Creation

The whole creation groans in pain
Travails in birth and burdened sore;
Its yearning felt in Autumn's shade,
In sky's expanse and ocean's roar,
Awaiting consummation's hour —
Christ's healing and transforming power.

In microscopic clarity
Each man of prayer may hear the call
Within the confines of the heart
Wherein is there reflected all —
All ecstasy, bliss and delight,
All sorrow, pain and darkest night.

In Christ's redeeming, suffering love
In which all men may share a part
There lies the reconciling power
With meditation's healing art
To share in His redeeming love
And His transfiguring passion prove.

The cosmic pain is finitude
And sin's decay and passion's lust;
Contingent powers long for release,
Perfection's hopes lie in the dust,
While on the dark horizon's line
Are signs of this world's last decline.

So men of God are drawn to prayer
By the indwelling Spirit's call,
And men of faith and love arise
Reversing thus the cosmic fall;
Redeeming man's aridity,
Renewing earth's fertility.

Further Reading

The following is a short bibliography of some of the recent major works concerned with the theological, philosophical and ethical themes which arise out of this anthology:

Agius, Ambrose, *God's Animals*, foreword by Cardinal Heenan (London: Catholic Study Circle for Animal Welfare, 1970).

Black, John, *Man's Dominion: The Search for Ecological Responsibility* (Edinburgh: Edinburgh University Press, 1970).

Carpenter, Edward and others, *Animals and Ethics* (London: Watkins Books, 1980 and Element Books, 1985).

Clark, Stephen R. L., *The Moral Status of Animals* (Oxford: Oxford University Press, 1977).

Granberg-Michaelson, Wesley (ed.), *Tending the Garden: Essays on the Gospel and the Earth* (Grand Rapids, Michigan: Wm. B. Erdmans, 1987).

Hart, John, *The Spirit of the Earth: A Theology of the Land* (New Jersey: Paulist Press, 1984).

Hume, C. W., *The Status of Animals in the Christian Religion* (London: Universities Federation for Animal Welfare, 1957).

Joranson, P. N. and Butigan, Ken (eds.), *Cry of the Environment: Rebuilding the Christian Creation Tradition* (Santa Fe, Mexico: Bear and Company, 1984).

Linzey, Andrew, *Christianity and the Rights of Animals* (London: SPCK, and New York: Crossroad, 1987).

—and Regan, Tom (eds.). *Compassion for Animals: Readings and Prayers* (London: SPCK 1988).

—and Regan, Tom (eds.), *Animals and Christianity: A Book of Readings* (London: SPCK, 1988).

—and Wexler, Peter J (eds.), *Heaven and Earth: Essex Essays in Theology and Ethics* (Worthing, Sussex: Churchman Publishing, 1986).

Magel, Charles R., *Keyguide to Information Sources in Animal Rights* (London: Manshall Publishing Limited, 1988).

McDonagh, Sean, *To Care for the Earth: A Call to a New Theology* (Dublin: Geoffrey Chapman, 1986).

McKenna, Virginia, Travers, Bill and Wray, Jonathan (eds.), *Beyond The Bars: The Zoo Dilemma* (Wellingborough, Northamptonshire, 1987).

Montefiore, Hugh (ed.), *Man and Nature* (London: Collins, 1975).

Regan, Tom, *The Case for Animal Rights* (Berkeley, California: University of California Press, 1983).

—*Animal Sacrifices: Religious Perspectives on the Use of Animals in Science* (Philadelphia: Temple University Press, 1986).

—*The Struggle for Animal Rights* (Philadelphia: International Society for Animal Rights, 1987).

—and Singer, Peter (eds.), *Animal Rights and Human Obligations* (New Jersey: Prentice-Hall, 1976),

Santmire, Paul, *The Travail of Nature: The Ambiguous Ecological Promise of Christian Theology* (Philadelphia: Fortress Press, 1985).

Singer, Peter, *Animal Liberation: A New Ethics for our Treatment of Animals* (London: Jonathan Cape, 1976).

Thomas, Keith, *Man and the Natural World: Changing Attitudes in England 1500–1800* (Harmondsworth: Penguin Books, 1984).

Wood, Barbara, *Our World, God's World* (London: Bible Reading Fellowship, 1986).

Wynne-Tyson, Jon (ed.), *The Extended Circle: A Dictionary of Humane Thought* (Fontwell, Sussex: Centaur Press, 1986).